Debunkum Beaver Pega CLSA Guide

Preparing for Pega CLSA 7.3/7.4 Certification (Book 1)

Copyright Notice

Disclaimer

The content within the publication is based solely on the
author's personal knowledge and experiences, and it does not represent any
other entities' views, either directly, or implied.

Readers' should view this publication as another point of view,
use it as a reference and sought their own conclusion.

Although the author and publisher
have made every effort to ensure that the
information in this book was correct at time of print,
the author and publisher do not assume and hereby disclaim any
liability to any party for any loss, damage, or disruption
caused by errors or omissions, whether such
errors or omissions result from
negligence, accident, or any
other causes.

The information in this book
is meant to supplement, not replace Pega Academy trainings.
Readers should ensure that they have completed the relevant Pega courses,
and to consult Pega Academy on matters related
to their trainings or certifications.

This is a non-official guide, and it is
created as a form of knowledge sharing, and presented as it is
without any warranties. Usage is entirely
at the reader's own risk.

By reading and using information in this
book, you signified your acceptance of these and assume all
responsibilities for its usage.

Dedication & Acknowledgements

First of all, I think we all need to thank
Alan Trefler, without him, there would not be the Pega
we are seeing today. It is also him, who kept Pega as a free company,
which was evident in the Reuters article on 'rather
eat sand than sell to other companies'.
Hopefully, Pega will continue
to be independent.

Special thanks to my dear wife
for the support provided for me to achieve
the CLSA certification, as well as the sacrificed family time
and encouragement she had provided me with to leverage on my academic
knowledge to contribute back to the community through this book.
Not to forget my boy, who volunteered to create a logo for
Debunkum Beaver, at the same time,
being my proof reader!

There were multiple great
SSAs/LSAs along my journey, who had
explained many important Pega concepts and guided
me in the past years. Their untiring explanations
and demonstrations are
greatly appreciated.

This book is a
dedication to all those who would
like to embark on the CLSA 7.3/7.4 Certifications.
With this, you now have one more
reliable resource.

Should I Buy This Book?

This is the first book of the Debunkum Beaver Pega CLSA Guide. Its focus is to help you to achieve the Pega CLSA certification.

If you do not know what is Pega CLSA, this book is not for you.

If you are not a Pega CSSA, this book is too advanced and not applicable to you 'yet' because it does not cover any basic of Pega. Check with Pega Academy on a suitable training program to get you started instead.

In short, the Debunkum Beaver Pega CLSA Guide is a series that aims to help you to achieve the Pega CLSA certification.

This series focus on how to tackle the CLSA exams, by treating you like a smart and knowledgeable student, one who is thirsty for knowledge.

The series also teaches you how to prepare and answer exam questions, without divulging any of the questions, lest say the answers themselves.

This is the first book of the Pega CLSA series, which lays the foundation for you to achieve Pega CLSA. This book is also a prerequisite for other books in this series.

If you are a Pega CSSA, planning to take the Pega CLSA Certification, this book is meant for you.

What this Book Is and Is Not

The purposes of this book are to:
- Act as a supplement to the existing Pega Academy trainings and Pega Community site
- Provide guidance on studying for the LSA Readiness exam, LSA Architecture exam, and LSA Architecture Application Build exam
- Provide personal suggestions on the approach for taking the LSA Architecture Application Build exam

This book DOES NOT:
- Replace any of the existing Pega Academy training information or any of its official sites
- Act as any official guide. This is just a personal sharing.
- Provide tips, sample questions or answers for your exams. You need to prepare it yourself, prove your worth and claim the accreditation all by yourself, which is what really makes this certification valuable, isn't it?

Please note that Pega CLSAs are bounded by the certification policies, thus, anyone claiming to provide you with questions/answers, scenario, etc. are just bunkums.

In summary, you need to use this book as a general guide for you to plan and take the relevant trainings from Pega Academy. If you do not study for it and depend solely on this book, you are bound to fail.

Contents

Preface

CLSA is the highest level of technical achievement in Pega. With the recent changes to this certification, the path of CLSA certification had become much more complicated.

In the past, you just need to pass a Pearson Vue exam (Part 1), followed by doing a 7-day application build (Part 2).

The new CLSA certification, consists of 3 parts, each having its own prerequisites, list of coverages, etc. Trying to comprehend the processes, plan for the various exams, and ultimately passing it, is much more difficult now.

This book is the 1st of the Pega CLSA series, titled: **Debunkum Beaver Pega CLSA Guide - Preparing for Pega CLSA 7.3/7.4 Certification (Book 1)**

The focus is on demystifying this certification, and most importantly, providing guidance and tips on how you could optimise your success rate.

Remember: Pega CLSA certification is not cheap! It makes a lot of sense for you to pass it on the 1st attempt!

Look out for more info at:
https://www.DebunkumBeaver.com

Author's Profile (Why Me?)

T he first question I would like to answer is "Why me?" This was also the first question I asked myself.

I am neither from Pega Academy nor had decades of Pega experiences. So, what made me qualified to write this book? Not to mention a book about the highest technical certification in Pega!

I Have Lecturing Experiences

I had delivered lectures and tutorials to students pursuing Master's and Bachelor's Degrees from Monash University and Deakin University, through their respective distance learning programs.

The largest student group that I had lectured was well over hundreds. Degree programs included the following:

- Bachelor of Information Technology
- Master of Information Technology
- Bachelor of Computing (Computer Science/Software Development)

This gave me knowledge and experience in handling undergraduates, their thought processes, and their common pitfalls.

I Have Experiences Writing Courseware

In case you do not know what a courseware is, it is similar to a full subject material offered in a university.

Courseware is not just the study or lecture materials, it included the tutorial exercises, sample solutions for the lecturers delivering the course, as well as the exam papers, with the associated marking schemes (rubric, as some might refer to it).

This experience provided me with great insights on the end-to-end structures of exams, it also provided me with a deeper understanding of what examiners are typically looking for, including the CLSA Team.

I am CLSA Certified in the New CLSA Path 7.3/7.4

There is no point in telling people how to prepare for Pega CLSA if one has not even passed it.

On top of that, being a CLSA does not mean that the person is qualified to teach. It should be the same new CLSA Path to have any relevance, shouldn't it?

Having decades of Pega expertise and experiences are commendable, but not relevant in writing this book because the exams structure is no longer the same.

In short, being certified in older versions of CLSA for many years, does not add more values compared to a person who had been through the new CLSA path, the same path that you would be taking, agree?

I Passed the Application Build on the 1st Attempt

Passing the Application Build on the 1st attempt, 2nd attempt, or even on the 3rd attempt, has no direct correlation to the technical skills.

However, the ability to pass it on the 1st attempt is an indication that the given candidate knows the approach and is inherently able to present his solution in the expected format. Coupled with my lecturing and courseware experiences, do you see the strong relevance now?

I Have a Strong Academic Background

I have a master's degree. During my masters, I had written thesis, published papers, and produced patents together with my professors and helped them to start up 2 companies, which were later bought over.

Therefore, writing books and doing publications are all in my blood.

I Have Experience Writing a Book

Writing a book is not easy. In general, it usually takes at least 6 months to complete a book, not including the miscellaneous tasks of getting a publisher, proof reading, book designing, and finally publishing it.

Worst, the return is often not worth the effort that one has put in. (Yes, I know Harry Potter, but that is more of a rare exception, rather than the norm. Furthermore, there is no way to disprove a fantasy series, is there?)

For me, it is not as difficult because this is not my first book. How hard could it be for me if I had possessed so many of the above attributes? All I need is just 1 month of my own free time to release a book.

I Have Many Years of IT Experiences

Apart from many years of IT experiences, I have experiences in other BPM/CRM systems as well as other areas, including SQL, UNIX, etc.

You may not be able to relate how these would help in passing the CLSA certification, but you would know the relevance after you have finished reading this book.

I Think There Should be More Pega Technical Books

Today, the biggest problem that Pega faced is a pool of certified and qualified Pega architects. It is not possible to further extend this pool of Pega architects if there are no books written for it. Take a look at Java, Oracle, Microsoft, CISCO, etc. There are tons of books on that and from various sources!

Today, the only relevant Pega related book in Amazon.com is only "Build for Change" – By Alan Trefler. However, that is more of a management book rather than a technical one.

Therefore, someone needs to start somewhere, and I am not shy to say that the best person is me; and doing a Pega CLSA Guide is a great starting point.

Summary: I Have Multiple Relevant Attributes

My boy wants to be a writer, just like me, and he is very motivated. At the age of 9, he had finished reading Sherlock Holmes (the original series).

The first question I asked him was: There are millions of books out there, why would anybody buy yours?

After I had set him on the thinking path, I suggested him to search for the author, read his profile in Wikipedia, and answer my question again.

With some guidance, he finally realised the reason: Sir Arthur Ignatius Conan Doyle is a physician by profession, which was why he could write Sherlock Holmes so convincingly!

His first novel, "The Haunted Grange of Goresthorpe", did not even get published, which goes back to the initial question to my boy: Anybody can write a book on a ghost story, why would anyone buy his?

In business terms, this is called "competitive advantage". A business or idea would prosper if and only if there is a "competitive advantage", coupled with a high entry barrier.

I had come across great professors with good academic accreditations, but their lectures were the best 'sleeping pills' one could ever buy in the open market!

Technical ability and knowledge are important. However, knowing the technicality and possessing the ability to solve the most complex issues do not give birth to good writers or good teachers --- these require a far more well-rounded ability to achieve that.

Are You Convinced?

I sincerely hope you are. If not, please don't get this book. I hate 'grumpies'. If you think you can do better by doing it solo, please feel free to do what you think is best for yourself.

Do I Need This Guide?

Pega does not provide any guidance on achieving the CLSA Certification. All it does is state the various prerequisites and the steps required to achieve it. Thus, there is a gap, as well as challenges, when one decided to embark on this certification.

Strictly speaking, without this guide, one can still pass the CLSA 7.3/7.4 Certification --- I am a living example.

However, I had spent a lot of time figuring things out, asked a lot of clarification questions to various people before finally understanding the certification path, prerequisites, the pitfalls, etc.

Thus, this guide is a compilation of the knowledge that I gained along the way, highlighting specific tricks that you can legally leverage on to improve your chance of passing this certification.

Of course, you could reinvent the wheel and go through the process, the pitfalls, retake the application build again and again... but bear in mind, as I shall remind you again, the Pega CLSA certification is not cheap. On top of that, you can only retake a maximum of 3 times per year, with specific intervals between each.

I had heard that for Pega 7.1 CLSA (possibly other earlier versions too), there were only 3 different scenarios, and once you had tried all, you cannot retake any further. Of course, how true that is, is irrelevant because the key point here is: Don't get yourself into that situation!

I had seen many people, with around 10 years of Pega experiences ended up in that situation --- practically doing the CLSA certification throughout their Pega careers, 5.x, 6.x, 7.1, now 7.3/7.4...

I just could not comprehend their thoughts, why should anyone torture themselves with that? Unless they really enjoy that...

Taking a step back, wouldn't it be better to just do it once, and do it good? I did, and I passed the application build on the 1st attempt.

Don't you think it is better to join me than them? ☺

Why Not Do This At Pega Community?

This is an interesting option that I had considered before. However, there are a few stoppers:

Limited and Lack of Control

I hate the feeling of being restricted. I have many ideas, plans and ways of doing things, but when there are people or situations that restrict or delay me, I get very pissed off.

Lack of Details

Pega Community is good but more often than not, the replies are just one-liner, link to other articles, and a bunch of description and steps, which would not help if you do not have good Pega knowledge in the first place. Interestingly, if you had that, you wouldn't need to go there to search for answer in the first place!

Do take note that I am not saying that Pega Community does not provide good information or solutions, it is just that it was not meant to teach and guide you like what you were taught in your undergraduate studies.

I Want To Teach and Have Students Who Want to Learn

The platform today, and possibly many years into the future, focuses on the technicality of how to do a task, not about the purpose, or the thought process that led to the solution, which is a crucial skill you would want to acquire if you want to pass the exams.

I needed a platform to allow me to do that, but in Pega Community, people have a stronger tendency to listen only to those 'renowned professional', who sometimes went down the 'too technical' path.

Therefore, there is basically no avenue that I could share the detailed and vast knowledge that I have.

Since I am an author, have the academic background, as well as a Pega CLSA, it makes perfect sense for me to do it through publication, thus, the birth of this book.

I want to teach, and if you want to learn, then welcome to the mind-blowing world of Debunkum Beaver! 😊

Part 1: The New 7.3/7.4 CLSA Certification

Overview

Firstly, to set the expectation right, I am not going to go into too much details on the new certification structure; anyway, the details are readily available at Pega website, which is always the most updated truth.

Secondly, I am sure you did not buy this book to be guided on how to read the information on the Pega website.

However, for completeness sake, I should still explain these here, and I will just highlight the key points.

In case of any discrepancies, please use the information on Pega website as the source of truth, as there may be changes after the publication of this book.

The URL is as follows:
https://academy.pega.com/Lead-System-Architect-Overview

Major Changes from Earlier Certifications

Prior to the new CLSA 7.3/7.4, the earlier CLSA certifications basically consisted of 2 parts:

- Theory exam, taken at Pearson VUE
- An Application Build, lasting 7 days in total

The new certification is more stringent, and it has 3 parts.

Firstly, you need to prove that you are ready to take this certification, followed by demonstrating that you can architect a Pega solution given any scenario.

Finally, able to demonstrate that you could build a solution, implement technical features, as well as able to analyse and solve technical issues (in which you are only given some users' observations during the exam).

The above requirements are all represented through the following exams. Therefore, to be a Pega CLSA, these are the 3 exams that you need to pass, in the given order:

- LSA Readiness exam, taken at Pearson VUE
- LSA Pega Architecture exam, also taken at Pearson VUE
- LSA Architecture Application Build Exam, administered by Pega

To complicate the certification, there are a long list of CLSA prerequisites that you need to clear in order to get the certification.

I had heard various discussions about whether the old CLSA certification or the new one is more difficult. These are all bunkums, which I, Debunkum Beaver, am here to debunk!

For example, one might feel that a 7-day Application Build is more challenging (since the duration is much longer), but don't forget, you have full knowledge and control of the design from the beginning till the end!

On the other hand, a 3-day Application Build might sound easy, but remember, you could be thrown any sort of application that you have no idea how it was built and designed in the first place.

Even though you may be familiar with the application, it could have been modified to create issues, as well as having some other rules removed. Thus, trying to understand and fix issues of the application is still time consuming and tedious.

On top of that, you only have 3 days for the build --- mistake in 1 day would cost you 33% of the exam time, while in the past, it was less than 15%!

If you throw any of the current CLSA into the other exams, many of them will fail. Not that they had forgotten or that they are not really qualified, but rather, the requirements and structures are all different.

In short, no matter what your technical level of Pega is, if you don't prepare, you will fail! No doubt about it! Therefore, let's not get involved in those stupid arguments and focus on getting yourself certified!

There is, however, one thing that is certain: The new CLSA Certification is going to take a much longer time to achieve, given the list of prerequisites and the long process as shown below.

Figure 1: CLSA Learning Path Overview (Image From Pega Site)

CLSA Prerequisites

Generally, I would say that the prerequisite for CLSA 7.3/7.4 is huge, compared with the earlier format.

The prerequisites are now divided into 2 parts, Required and Suggested:

Required
- Certified System Architect (CSA) certification - in any version
- Certified Senior System Architect (CSSA) certification - in any version
- Customer Service Ready badge
- Pega Platform Ready badge
- Certified Pega Decisioning Consultant (CPDC) certification - in any version

Suggested
- Robotic Automation Ready badge
- Completion of Implementing Pega Robotics course

If you had been following the CLSA certification for some time, or had made a copy of the list before, you will realise that the list had changed!

In particular, the CSPMC was removed (retired), and there is a new "Suggested" section, which contains Robotic specific knowledge.

LSA Readiness Exam

The LSA Readiness exam is the first exam in the CLSA certification path and focuses on configuration of Pega applications.

The following is a quick rundown on this exam.

Tests knowledge learned:
- In the listed Prerequisites
- SSA Advanced Topics
- Pega Help
- PDN
- Project implementation real-life experience

Exam format
- Two-hour standard exam that is delivered at Pearson VUE testing centres
- Passing score of 65% (Subject to change without notice)
- Exam blueprint is available at Pega Academy
- Exam information and the Study Guide are available at the Pearson VUE site

The SSA Advanced Topics are as follows:

- Customizing Security Requirements in Pega Applications
- Configuring Agent Processing
- Customizing the User Experience
- Improving Application Performance
- Creating Mobile Solutions

The SSA Advanced Topics was introduced to help system architects to fill potential gaps in knowledge and experience, given that each person has different project implementation opportunities.

LSA Architecture Exam

B efore taking this exam, you should have completed the Lead System Architect Course.

This is a 2-hours standard exam that is delivered at Pearson VUE testing centres. You need to achieve 65% (Subject to change without notice) in order to pass.

If you take a closer look at the prerequisite of this exams, you will notice that the CPDC certification is a prerequisite for this exam, not the LSA Readiness exam.

In other words, you could take the LSA Readiness exam before taking the CPDC certification.

LSA Architecture Application Build

The LSA Architecture Application Build (sometimes simply referred as "LSA Application Build"), is the final exam to achieve the Pega CLSA Certification.

Interestingly, even if you had cleared the other 2 exams, there would be no indication of your progress in PDN. This is the last hurdle, so make your best effort to clear it asap!

The following are some quick points regarding this build:

- Provided with Pre-built Pega 7 application
- Analyze key areas of the current design and identify architectural deficiencies
- Implement extensible and reusable solutions for new requirements
- Identify problem areas and take corrective actions with the current application
- Document your analysis and solutions using a supplied documentation template

- 3 consecutive days and requires a score of 70% in order to pass

You could be given 3 to 6 questions for this application build. Each of the questions could entail a separate starting application or that you could be required to create one from scratch.

In general, every question is independent of one another and you are expected to package each solution as individual package, with no dependency.

Please refer to the official information for any updates.

Conclusion

As you can see, Pega CLSA 7.3/7.4 entails a lot more than the earlier certification, and it definitely requires more time and effort to prepare and achieve it.

Now that you understand the 3 exams and the prerequisites, the next step is to understand how to prepare for it!

Part 2: Preparing Pega CLSA 7.3/7.4 Certification

Introduction

In this section, we will focus on preparing you for the CLSA 7.3/7.4 certification.

For simplicity and ease of your preparation, this chapter is divided into sections that directly correspond to the ACTUAL exams that you need to take.

This would make it easier for you to see what is required for each exam and track your CLSA certification journey as progressive achievements accordingly.

In the most simplified form, there are only 3 exams to take:
- LSA Readiness Exam
- LSA Architecture Exam
- LSA Architecture Application Build

Preparing for LSA Readiness Exam

This is technically a pretty simple exam, not much magic here. The challenge is basically that there is vast amount of materials that you need to read through.

To pass this, all you need is basically to complete the list of self-study courses, memorise the information, and you are ready to go.

You should not have much issue for this exam, unless you are truly not ready yet… 😐

Use the LSA Study Guide

I have seen candidates, who just based their studies on the list of prerequisites listed at the following Pega Academy URL:

https://academy.pega.com/library/74/lead-system-architect-readiness-exam

Well, those are not enough!

As a first step, you should get a copy of the Study Guide, and use it as the base for your preparation. As of this writing, the Study Guide is available at the following URL:
https://home.pearsonvue.com/Clients/Pegasystems/LSA_study_guide.aspx

In case the link changes, you can always Google for it.

The most important part of the Study Guide is a list of links that points you to the knowledge that you should learn. The following is a screenshot of that document:

Pega Academy

As an LSA Candidate, you already completed courses to prepare for the CSA and CSSA exams. Depending on the amount of time that has passed since earning your certification and the course version, you may want to review the current course (including exercises) to ensure you are familiar with the current product.

The links to following self-study courses will help you prepare:

- System Architect Essentials: https://academy.pega.com/enroll/C-1125
- Senior System Architect: https://academy.pega.com/enroll/C-916
- Pega Customer Service Foundation: https://academy.pega.com/enroll/C-798
- Implementing Pega Customer Service: https://academy.pega.com/enroll/C-933
- Pega Decisioning Consultant: https://academy.pega.com/enroll/C-1155

Not all Pega projects expose Senior System Architects to the same product features and releases. Therefore, Pega Academy provides self-study courses to help you fill in gaps between your unique field experience and expected product knowledge.

The following 7.3 self-study courses help you fill those gaps:

- Customizing Security Requirements in Pega Applications: https://academy.pega.com/enroll/C-817
- Customizing the User Experience: https://academy.pega.com/enroll/C-865
- Configuring Agent Processing: https://academy.pega.com/enroll/C-859
- Improving Application Performance: https://academy.pega.com/enroll/C-885
- Creating Mobile Solutions: https://academy.pega.com/enroll/C-807

The Pega Platform Help File

LSA candidates are expected to keep their skills current. LSA candidates need to understand the features and functions of each Pega Platform release. If you earned your CSSA on an earlier version of the Pega Platform, make sure to spend time reviewing the Platform "What's New" in the Pega Community: https://community1.pega.com/sites/pdn.pega.com/files/help_v73/procomhelpmain.htm

Figure 2: LSA Readiness Exam Study Guide Sample

The tricky part of this exam is that the coverage is HUGE. It is highly likely that after you had completed all the materials, you had forgotten about what you learnt earlier. To address this, always make it a good practice to keep notes of all your studies.

New Exam Question Format

The exam is conducted at Pearson VUE, where the format is similar to the other certifications, with some subtle differences:

CPDC (Certified Pega Decisioning Consultant) Exam
Type of Exam: 63 question multiple choice exam

LSA Readiness Exam (CLSA Certification Path)
Type of Exam: 60-question exam, including multiple choice and drag & drop questions

Figure 3: New Exam Question Format

Note that there is now a new type of question format: "drag & drop questions".

If you had done other exams before (e.g. from Oracle, Microsoft, CISCO, etc), you will know that this means that you might be given a number of choices for a given questions, and you need to drag all the applicable choices to a given area; and depending on the question itself, you might need to sort them in the correct order.

To address this type of questions, make sure that during your study, pay extra attention to any information that requires a specific ordering of steps to complete.

Although in a real-world scenario some of the order might not be important, you may still be expected to present it in the expected order that you have been taught.

Where Should You Start?

In general, always use the reference links provided. Even if you are certified in a minor version earlier, always go through the EXACT version provided in the reference links again!

Newbies

If you are a newbie or someone with a lot of time, I would advise you to study according to the order presented in the LSA Study Guide.

Start with the Pega Academy Courses:
- System Architect Essentials
- Senior System Architect
- Pega Customer Service Foundation
- Implementing Pega Customer Service
- Pega Decisioning Consultant

Then the SSA Advanced Topics:
- Customizing Security Requirements in Pega Applications
- Customizing the User Experience

- Configuring Agent Processing
- Improving Application Performance
- Creating Mobile Solutions

Followed by the list of help files.

Experts With Limited Time

First of all, you need to understand there is a risk if you are going to focus on certain topics instead of others.

On the other hand, if you know yourself well, then it would not be efficient for you to spent too much time on topics that you are an expert in.

The first step is to read through the fine lines of the CLSA certifications, which stated:

"However, recognizing that each person has different project implementation opportunities, Pega Academy is introducing self-paced courses that help system architects fill potential gaps in knowledge and experience."

Those were the introduction lines given for the SSA Advanced Topics, so your focus is to ensure that you are up to that level for all the topics listed there.

Next step would be to go through the Pega Academy courses. You could possibly do a quick run through of the "System Architect Essentials" but focus more on the "Senior System Architect".

The reason is that if you are a good SSA and knows the basic of Pega, then you would not have any problem doing the "Senior System Architect" directly without revising the "System Architect Essentials".

After that, do the rest of the courses: "Pega Customer Service Foundation", "Implementing Pega Customer Service", and "Pega Decisioning Consultant".

Depending on your proficiency in those and the version that you are certified in, spend appropriate amount of time on those.

Next, do a quick browse of the help files. I would not recommend you to memory any information there, as there is simply too much information. Just make sure you browse through and understand those.

Lastly, go through the SSA Advanced Topics once again. You might have forgotten stuff over there!

In summary, this is what I suggest for an expert:
1) SSA Advanced Topics
2) Senior System Architect, (for SAE, just use it as a reference or do the practice exam)
3) Do other courses, such as: "Pega Customer Service Foundation", "Implementing Pega

Customer Service", and "Pega Decisioning Consultant"

4) Browse through the help files (if you are hard-pressed for time, then do a quick one)
5) Do the SSA Advanced Topics again

Once again, this 'express path' entails risk and you should assess your capability appropriately.

Exams are largely the same format as other Pega certifications, except that there are now drag-and-drop questions. You need to select from a list, and most of the time, you must present it in the correct order. Therefore, while doing the studies, if there are specific steps, memorise them. In real life, some steps may not need to be in any specific order; however, in the exams, make sure you remember the order that you have been taught.

Remember, no matter how well you know the various topics or how recent your version is, make it a point that you read the EXACT version given in the link.

By default, read it in the given order. The Help Files are huge, you may not be able to cover all.

Preparing for LSA Architecture Exam

B efore taking this exam, make sure that you have completed the Lead System Architect Course. In fact, if you look at the prerequisite for the Pega Architecture exam, you will notice the following:

- LSA Readiness Exam passed attempt (any version)
- CPDC certification (any version)
- Lead System Architect course (7.3-7.4)

Although this is the time where your CPDC certification is required, you may still wish to get your CPDC during your Readiness exam since the study material is also listed there.

Passing mark is 65% (Subject to change without notice). 65% seems to be on the low side compared with other Pega certifications. Trust me, it is not easy to achieve the 65%.

I had heard people comparing the CLSA 7.1 Part 1 with those of the new CLSA 7.3/7.4 exams. The comment is generally that CLSA 7.1 Part 1 is more difficult than the Readiness exam, while the Architecture exam is the most difficult among the 3.

I had also heard some saying that Architecture exam is easier.

My view is that it really depends. If you had been doing a lot of implementations with 7.3/7.4, including those advanced topics, **under the guidance of a good LSA**, then Architecture Exam would be easier for you.

However, if you had been hacking Pega to achieve your customers' requirements, then the Architecture Exam will be very difficult for you.

Specifically, there are a lot of pitfalls created specially to catch those 'naughty SSA'.

Therefore, when you read through the Lead System Architect Course, reflect to what you had been doing before, and then think about how you would have implemented it differently given the information in the course.

If your approach is going to be drastically different, my advice is for you to bring it up to the instructor and discuss the pros and cons of your approach.

In general, remember to review the information in the Lead System Architect Course, including those exercises, and make sure you complete all of those.

When I first took the Lead System Architect Course, the information and the exercises were still very crude.

In short, even if you followed the exercise steps, you will not be able to accomplish the exercises! ☹

However, do not stop there, load the sample exercises and walkthrough the instructions to understand how those are implemented.

With the recent revisions to the study materials, I believe it should be better now.

After completing the Lead System Architect Course, take note of the features mentioned within, launch the VM and try out the features yourself. Make sure you know how to use those. You need to have a working knowledge to pass.

Exams are largely the same format as other Pega certifications, except that there are now drag-and-drop questions. You need to select from a list, and most of the time, you must present it in the correct order. Therefore, while doing the studies, if there are specific steps, memorise them. In real life, some steps may not need to be in any specific order; however, in the exams, make sure you remember the order that you have been taught.

Preparing for LSA Architecture Application Build

F irst of all, don't underestimate the difficulty of this. I can assure you that you will not have enough time!

Therefore, you need to prepare as much as you can beforehand! Especially your laptop and VM, make sure that they are in proper condition!

Much of this book focused on preparing for the Application Build, which many candidates simply ignored the importance of getting yourself FULLY ready before the exam starts!

A lot of candidate simply spent too much time reviewing materials, learning how to implement certain features, and ended up overlooked the fact that you have far more to prepare than those technical details.

Get a Copy of CLSA 7.3_7.4 App Build Exam Preparation Guide

When you are at this stage, the first thing that you need to do is to get a copy of the **CLSA 7.3_7.4 App Build Exam Preparation Guide v1.0.pdf**.

As of this writing, you can get it from the following URL:
https://community1.pega.com/system/files/CLSA%207.3_7.4%20App%20Build%20Exam%20Preparation%20Guide%20v1.0.pdf

The following is a screenshot of the document:

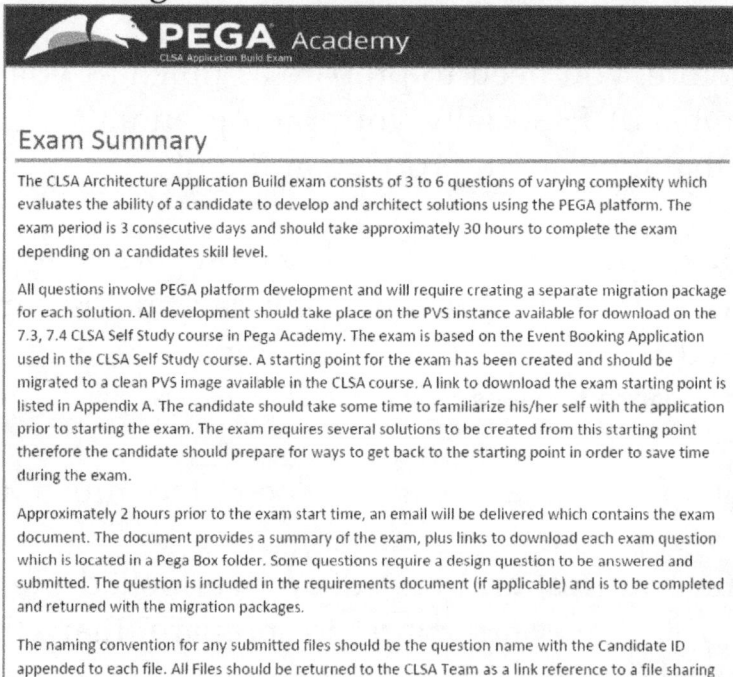

PEGA Academy
CLSA Application Build Exam

Exam Summary

The CLSA Architecture Application Build exam consists of 3 to 6 questions of varying complexity which evaluates the ability of a candidate to develop and architect solutions using the PEGA platform. The exam period is 3 consecutive days and should take approximately 30 hours to complete the exam depending on a candidates skill level.

All questions involve PEGA platform development and will require creating a separate migration package for each solution. All development should take place on the PVS instance available for download on the 7.3, 7.4 CLSA Self Study course in Pega Academy. The exam is based on the Event Booking Application used in the CLSA Self Study course. A starting point for the exam has been created and should be migrated to a clean PVS image available in the CLSA course. A link to download the exam starting point is listed in Appendix A. The candidate should take some time to familiarize his/her self with the application prior to starting the exam. The exam requires several solutions to be created from this starting point therefore the candidate should prepare for ways to get back to the starting point in order to save time during the exam.

Approximately 2 hours prior to the exam start time, an email will be delivered which contains the exam document. The document provides a summary of the exam, plus links to download each exam question which is located in a Pega Box folder. Some questions require a design question to be answered and submitted. The question is included in the requirements document (if applicable) and is to be completed and returned with the migration packages.

The naming convention for any submitted files should be the question name with the Candidate ID appended to each file. All Files should be returned to the CLSA Team as a link reference to a file sharing

Figure 4: CLSA 7.3_7.4 App Build Exam Preparation Guide v1.0

In general, you could be given 3 to 6 questions for this exam. It would take approximately 30 hours to complete the exam.

In other words, you are expected to spend 10 hours per day. Therefore, you should not schedule any other tasks during this period. However, it is highly likely, or rather, a certainty, that you will need to spend more time than that for this exam.

No matter how many questions you are given, always use the estimated hours for each question to pace yourself. For example, if you have 6 questions, with estimated time as follows:
    Q1: 7 hours;
    Q2: 3 hours;
    Q3: 6 hours;
    Q4: 4 Hours;
    Q5: 7 hours;
    Q6: 3 hours

Then you should aim to completed Q1 and Q2 on Day 1; Q3 and Q4 on Day 2; Q5 and Q6 on Day 3.

In the CLSA 7.3_7.4 App Build Exam Preparation Guide, there is a link to a starting point application. You should download it first to familiar yourself with the application.

When you are ready to take the LSA Architecture Application Build, you need to register for the Application build by dropping an email to:

CLSATeam@pega.com

Register As Early As You Can

The moment you know that you are going to take the Application Build, just go ahead and register for a date first.

This is because the CLSA Team will acknowledge your registration and reply an email containing several instructions.

Read the Email Carefully for Any Last-Minute Updates

Firstly, they would advise you on the VM that they would be using for grading, which generally would be the VM in the Pega Self-Study course. If you do not have access to that VM, you can contact them to obtain one.

Open All Attachments and Review Them

Next, the email will contain attachments detailing the configuration of the VM, including the usernames and passwords, configuration files location, configuration of various supporting tools including Database client, Putty, FTP client, SMA, as well as common DB commands for starting and stopping the DB server.

On top of that, there are also instructions on how to resolve a corrupted search index.

Test and Configure Your VM As Soon As You Can

As you can see, there are a lot of preparation that you need to do and be familiar with before the exam starts. So, do that as soon as you can.

Given that there are a lot of tasks to complete before the Application Build, it would not be wise for you to register for the exam just a day before!

Many people I know took things too lightly and assumed everything were in order and started the exam without due preparation.

In the end, they had to spend a lot of unnecessary time on setting up the connectivity and fixing VM issues. Please don't be one of them.

In the later sections, I will share with you the details of those configurations, some of which I used my own procedure rather than those in the provided document (for obvious reasons).

Know How to Reschedule

If there are any unforeseen circumstances, you can always reschedule your Application Build.

Remember, **If you really need to reschedule, please give the CLSA Team at least 24-hours notice prior to the exam start date**.

More details and updates are available in the acknowledgement email.

Choosing a Good Starting Time

The Application Build exam is automated. So, you are free to choose any date and time.

Remember to choose a time that is most convenient for you. You do not have to be bounded by working hours or holidays. If you are a 'night owl', feel free to start the exam at 11pm or whatever time you desired.

Most importantly, make sure that you can fully focus on the build without any disturbance for your selected exam period.

Be Wise on the Selection of the Time

Assume that you decided to follow the normal working hours for your Application Build exam, where you start work at 9am. What would you set the exam start time to be? 9a.m.?

NO, DON'T do that! You should set it as 11am instead!

The reason is because the question paper will be sent to you 2 hours before your elected time, in this case, it would be at 7am, which most likely you are not even ready to read it yet!

Therefore, by choosing your starting time wisely, you would have given yourself another 2 more precious hours.

Trust me, every minute counts for this Application Build!

Fix the Inherent Issue with the VM

Too many candidates assumed that everything is ready for them when the Application Build starts.

They assumed it is the responsibility of the examiners to ensure all these. Nothing is further from the truth. It is always the candidate's responsibility.

Before the publication of this book, I did a quick check. The VM that is in the Pega Academy is still the one that I used recently: LSA_731_VM_20171026.ova.

VM has Out-Of-Memory Issue

This VM has an inherent Out Of Memory issue.

Try starting the VM, then leave it there for a few hours, and you will get this error message:

```
Pega 7 Exercise Environment started on
Allow 3-4 minutes after starting before attempting to access Pega 7
To access Pega 7, open a browser of your choice and enter the URL:
      http://
pega7 login Out of memory: Kill process 1402 (java) score 500 or sacrifice chil
d
Killed process 1402, UID 501, (java) total-vm:743703ZkB, anon-rss:4516736kB, fil
e-rss:664kB
```

Figure 5: VM Out-Of-Memory Error Message

If you are not aware of this issue, you will encounter a situation where Designer Studio suddenly stopped responding during your Application Build.

Interestingly, you might ask: "Why in the hell would anybody even bother to test that?"

Well, that is my character, I tend to double check and ensure all the information and resources are in place before I start.

Even in a real-world scenario, I would check the validity of all assumptions before my exam starts --- Start the VM, leave it overnight and come back to check for issues in the morning! This is what we called "smoke test".

Can you imagine how devastating it would be when your VM kept crashing while you are doing the exam? Not only would it be demoralising, it would also cast great doubts on your solution, thinking that your solution caused the crash!

Fixing the Issue

Before the Application Build, I had checked with the CLSA Team and confirmed this issue. They also confirmed that the fix is to increase the memory to 8GB.

Of course, you could create your own VM that is super optimised and able to run on lower memory but bear in mind the additional time that you need to spend on all those.

Worst, the examiners are not going to use your VM, they are going to baseline using the one provided in the Pega Academy!

What Type of Machine(s) Do You Need

You have studied hard for the exams and paid hundreds or even thousands to get this certification, so do yourself a favour: Get a good machine(s)!

My Recommended Machine Specs
Given that the exam VM required at least 8GB, your laptop should be at least 12GB. This is my standard for running a VM --- always leave a margin of at least 4GB, which would still allow me to run standard apps in the host, such as Outlook email, Words document, etc.

However, I have heard that 12GB machine might still be a struggle, therefore, it is best to have at least 16GB to run the exam VM.

But sadly, a 16GB machine is not going to make things easy for you. Get a machine with at least 20GB RAM.

Please note that I am not here to override the minimum specifications for the exam, I am just suggesting a specification that will give you lesser headache.

You could still proceed with the exams by allocating only 6GB to the VM, but just be aware of the issue above. I am sure you will not want to have Out Of Memory error in your exam!

Personally, I would strongly suggest that you get a better machine, it will save you a lot of trouble during the application build --- trust me.

Alternative Option
If you could not get the specs above, get 2 machines instead.

If 16GB is enough for the application build, why am I asking you to have 2 such machines?

The reason is simple: Unless you have a super photographic memory, which I don't, you would need to be able to refer to the LSA Course VM in parallel during your application build.

Anyway, if the information taught in the Lead System Architect Course is of 'no use' for the exam, why would you even attend that training in the first place?

Therefore, if you only have 1 machine, then you need at least 20GB to run 2 VMs at the same time.

Disk Space Recommendation

For my exam, I moved out my rarely used VMs, till I have around 100GB of free diskspace. Strictly speaking, you do not need that much.

I would say 30GB of free diskspace would be sufficient. This amount of diskspace is not needed to run the VM, but you will need it for making backups and snapshots.

Do Multiple Snapshots of the Exercise Solutions

After you have done the LSA Course, make sure you have a snapshot of all the practice exercises, which would then allow you to revert back to a specific exercise to look at the code at that point.

Strictly speaking, it is not critical, but I did. As mentioned, I do not have a photographic memory, thus, I need to get ready all these additional things before the exam to make it easier for me to refer.

This is an example of the snapshot that I made for the Lead System Architect Course VM:

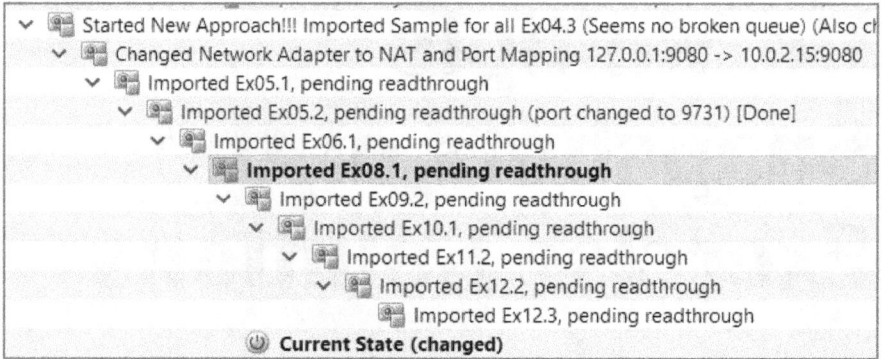

```
∨  🖳 Started New Approach!!! Imported Sample for all Ex04.3 (Seems no broken queue) (Also ch
   ∨  🖳 Changed Network Adapter to NAT and Port Mapping 127.0.0.1:9080 -> 10.0.2.15:9080
      ∨  🖳 Imported Ex05.1, pending readthrough
         ∨  🖳 Imported Ex05.2, pending readthrough (port changed to 9731) [Done]
            ∨  🖳 Imported Ex06.1, pending readthrough
               ∨  🖳 Imported Ex08.1, pending readthrough
                  ∨  🖳 Imported Ex09.2, pending readthrough
                     ∨  🖳 Imported Ex10.1, pending readthrough
                        ∨  🖳 Imported Ex11.2, pending readthrough
                           ∨  🖳 Imported Ex12.2, pending readthrough
                              🖳 Imported Ex12.3, pending readthrough
      🕘 Current State (changed)
```

Figure 6: Snapshot Of Lead System Architect Course VM

I know it may seem ridiculous to some readers, but to me, my objective is simple: I DO NOT want to take any unnecessary risk! Therefore, I am taking all the precautional steps that I could.

Can you relate the purpose of a machine with at least 20GB or 2 machines with at least 16GB each now?

With a single 20GB machine or two 16GB machines, you should be able to run these 2 VMs independently, one for the LSA Course, the other for your actual application build.

If you don't have the above, I would suggest that you go and loan it, or buy it.

Modify the DB Setup Instructions

The documents that CLSA Team sent you will contain instructions to create DB connections. Those are great, but there is a potential issue - you will have a problem if your VM's IP changes.

This will happen if you changed your network settings or connect through another network. If you cannot guarantee that you would be in the same network throughout the whole exam, or cannot confirm that your IP will not change, it is better to follow the instruction below instead.

There are 2 parts to setting up the DB connection to the VM:
- Update PostgreSQL Default Settings
- Update Host-Based Authentication Default Settings

Update PostgreSQL Default Settings
Sadly, if you are unfamiliar with UNIX, trying to do this would be a mission impossible for you. I will try my best to give you step-by-step instruction and

guidance. When you startup the VM, you will get the following screen once the VM is started:

```
Pega 7 Exercise Environment started on ▮▮▮▮▮▮▮▮ at ▮▮▮▮▮▮

Allow 3-4 minutes after starting before attempting to access Pega 7

To access Pega 7, open a browser of your choice and enter the URL:

        http://▮▮▮▮▮▮▮▮▮▮▮:9080

pega7 login: _
```

Figure 7: VM Screen After Startup

Login using the following:
Login Name: *root*
Password: *install*

Once you have logged in, you will see the following "Last login:" info as follows:

```
pega7 login: root
Password:
Last login: ▮▮▮▮▮▮▮▮▮▮▮▮▮▮ on tty1
[root@pega7 ~]# _
```

Figure 8: Command Prompt After Login

> *If your mouse is 'locked' in the VM, look for this image at the bottom of the VM dialog and press the command shown there. In my case, it is to press the "Ctrl" and "Alt" key together.*
>
> `Ctrl + Alt`

> *I am using Oracle Virtual Box, you are free to use VMWare. However, the free version of the VMWare is VMWare Player, which does not allow you to do snapshot! Therefore, I do not recommend you to use VMWare for the exam!*

There are 2 files that you need to modify:
```
postgresql.conf
pg_hba.conf
```

The provided document mentioned that those are in the following location:

```
/var/lib/pgsql/9.3/data/
```

Sadly, the provided instruction has not been updated to reflect the actual path in the VM... ☹

That is why, I had told you to prepare all these as earlier as possible. If you do, you could at least be able to send an email to ask them.

Nevertheless, it is always better to equip yourself with more knowledge, including knowledge that is beyond Pega itself. In this case, some UNIX commands.

The best way out of this is to use the "find" command to look for the file, as follows:

```
find / -name "postgresql.conf"
```

The following is the screenshot:

```
[root@pega7 ~]# find / -name "postgresql.conf"
/var/lib/pgsql/9.4/data/postgresql.conf
```

Figure 9: New Location for the DB Configuration Files

From the output, you can see that the file is now located in:

```
/var/lib/pgsql/9.4/data
```

Obviously, the database had been upgraded, but the instructions had not! I sincerely hope that they would have updated it by now.

The next thing is to open that file and edit it. Depending on your preference, you can choose whatever editor you like to edit the file. I am from "old school", so I prefer to use "vi" to edit.

Another reason for me to stick to the vi Editor is that this tool is almost guaranteed to be in all variances of UNIX.

The command to edit the 1st file is as follows:

```
vi /var/lib/pgsql/9.4/data/postgresql.conf
```

The following is the screenshot:

```
[root@pega? ~]# vi /var/lib/pgsql/9.4/data/postgresql.conf
```

Figure 10: Command to Edit "postgresql.conf" File

After you have pressed [Enter], make sure you can see something like the following:

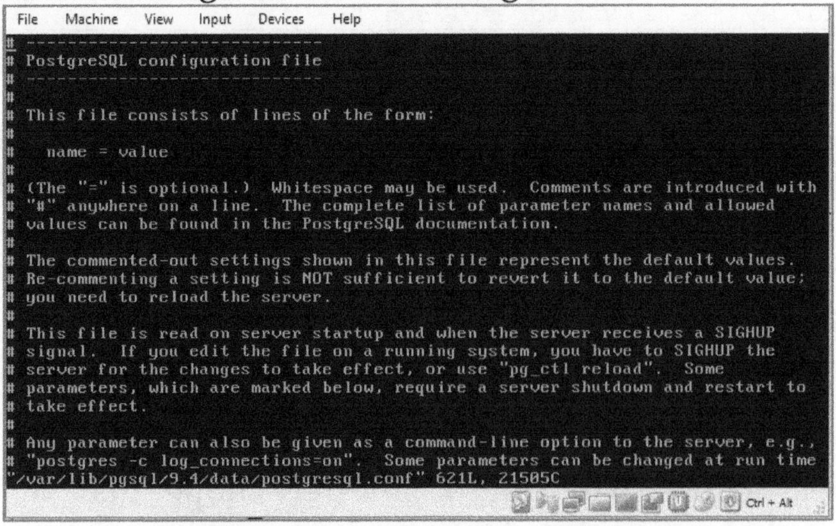

Figure 11: Initial "postgresql.conf" File

If you do not see something like the above, you might have typed the wrong name, and created a new file instead. To exit this, press the 5 key sequences below:
[Esc][Esc][:][q][!]

This will bring you back to the command prompt. You can press the [UP] & [DOWN] arrow keys to review the earlier commands and then use your [LEFT] & [RIGHT] arrow keys to move back and forth along the command line and edit it accordingly.

Pressing the [Esc] key twice is generally not necessary, but it is always a best practice when using vi. The problem with vi is that some commands depends on the current context, so by pressing [Esc] twice, you are always back to the "base" command context.

vi Editor is very powerful, but this book is not a primer for that, you can always google for more commands and tricks, however, I will teach you to use the most basic commands, in its simplest form because you job is to pass CLSA, not to be an UNIX expert!

The next step is to edit the relevant section of this file.

Press [Esc][Esc], followed by the down arrow to scroll the file, until you see the "CONNECTIONS AND AUTHENTICATION" section as shown below.

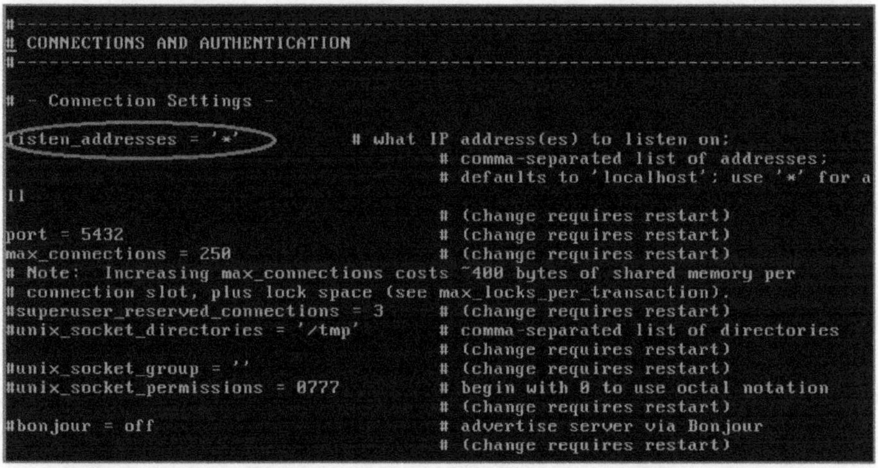
```
#------------------------------------------------------------------------------
# CONNECTIONS AND AUTHENTICATION
#------------------------------------------------------------------------------

# - Connection Settings -

listen_addresses = '*'          # what IP address(es) to listen on;
                                        # comma-separated list of addresses;
                                        # defaults to 'localhost'; use '*' for a
ll
                                        # (change requires restart)
port = 5432                             # (change requires restart)
max_connections = 250                   # (change requires restart)
# Note:  Increasing max_connections costs ~400 bytes of shared memory per
# connection slot, plus lock space (see max_locks_per_transaction).
#superuser_reserved_connections = 3     # (change requires restart)
#unix_socket_directories = '/tmp'       # comma-separated list of directories
                                        # (change requires restart)
#unix_socket_group = ''                 # (change requires restart)
#unix_socket_permissions = 0777         # begin with 0 to use octal notation
                                        # (change requires restart)
#bonjour = off                          # advertise server via Bonjour
                                        # (change requires restart)
```
Figure 12: Connections and Authentication Section of PostgreSQL.conf

vi also has command for you to find a text in the current file, you can always google for the command!

The Circled part is the area that you should change. Basically, it is just to remove the "#" in front of that line, which basically uncomment that line and make the statement: `listen_addresses = '*'` in force.

To delete the "#", move your mouse to the given character and press the "x" key ONCE. Which will delete that character.

The next tricky thing is to save this file. In vi, do the following 6 key sequences:

```
[Esc][Esc][:][w][q][!]
```

Recall:
To exit without saving:
[Esc][Esc][:][q][!]
To exit with saving:
[Esc][Esc][:][w][q][!]

The difference is just the [w] key in the sequence.

Back at the command prompt, to validate that you have indeed made that change, you can use the UNIX "cat" command.

To do that, when you are back at the command prompt, press the [UP] arrow. This will show you the earlier "vi" command with the file that you just edited.

Using the [LEFT] arrow, move to the "vi" command and change it to "cat", but before you press [ENTER], go back to the end of the command and add in: " | grep listen_addresses"

The command that you need to execute to check the changes is as follows:

```
cat  /var/lib/pgsql/9.3/data/postgresql.conf  |  grep
listen_addresses
```

The following is the screenshot of the output:

```
[root@pega7 ~]# cat /var/lib/pgsql/9.4/data/postgresql.conf | grep listen_addres
ses
listen_addresses = '*'          # what IP address(es) to listen on;
[root@pega7 ~]#
```

Figure 13: Check That postgresql.conf File Is Updated

Take note that the echo from the command shows that the new "listen_addresses" line does not have the "#" anymore.

> *Alternatively, you can use the same vi command to open the file, scroll down and look at the changes to confirm.*

The next task is to edit the 2nd file.

Update Host-Based Authentication Default Settings

The host-based authentication is represented in the pg_hba.conf file.

Many tips are given when edited the 1st file, thus I am not going to repeat those again. You should edit the 1st file before this. Not that it matters, but you should be familiar with the tips first. Please note that I do not want to treat you like babies, but I still have to treat you like my students.

The pg_hba.conf is located in the same location as the earlier postgresql.conf.

Use a text editor (I am using vi in my example), and open the file, you should see the following:

```
# PostgreSQL Client Authentication Configuration File
# ====================================================
#
# Refer to the "Client Authentication" section in the PostgreSQL
# documentation for a complete description of this file.  A short
# synopsis follows.
#
# This file controls: which hosts are allowed to connect, how clients
# are authenticated, which PostgreSQL user names they can use, which
# databases they can access.  Records take one of these forms:
#
# local      DATABASE  USER    METHOD  [OPTIONS]
# host       DATABASE  USER    ADDRESS METHOD  [OPTIONS]
# hostssl    DATABASE  USER    ADDRESS METHOD  [OPTIONS]
# hostnossl  DATABASE  USER    ADDRESS METHOD  [OPTIONS]
#
# (The uppercase items must be replaced by actual values.)
#
# The first field is the connection type: "local" is a Unix-domain
# socket, "host" is either a plain or SSL-encrypted TCP/IP socket,
# "hostssl" is an SSL-encrypted TCP/IP socket, and "hostnossl" is a
# plain TCP/IP socket.
#
# DATABASE can be "all", "sameuser", "samerole", "replication", a
"/var/lib/pgsql/9.4/data/pg_hba.conf" 92L, 4306C
```

Figure 14: Sample pg_hba.conf File

Use the [DOWN] arrow to scroll through the file, until you see something like the following:

```
# Put your actual configuration here
# ----------------------------------
#
# If you want to allow non-local connections, you need to add more
# "host" records.  In that case you will also need to make PostgreSQL
# listen on a non-local interface via the listen_addresses
# configuration parameter, or via the -i or -h command line switches.

# TYPE  DATABASE        USER            ADDRESS                 METHOD
```

Figure 15: Section of the pg_hba.conf to Edit

For each of the column in the diagram above, you are supposed to enter a value. In this situation, you need to add a whole new line, as follows:

```
Host   all    all    0.0.0.0/0    trust
```

You can use [TAB] key to separate and align them nicely (although not necessary). The modified section will look like the following:

```
# Put your actual configuration here
# ----------------------------------
#
# If you want to allow non-local connections, you need to add more
# "host" records.  In that case you will also need to make PostgreSQL
# listen on a non-local interface via the listen_addresses
# configuration parameter, or via the -i or -h command line switches.


# TYPE  DATABASE        USER            ADDRESS               METHOD
# Added by
host    all             all             0.0.0.0/0             trust
# "local" is for Unix domain socket connections only
local   all             all                                   trust
# IPv4 local connections:
host    all             all             127.0.0.1/32          trust
host    all             all             10.0.0.0/8            md5

# IPv6 local connections:
host    all             all             ::1/128               reject
# Allow replication connections from localhost, by a user with the
```

Figure 16: Sample Updated pg_hba.conf

Save the edited file, confirm the changes are in effect and exit the editor.

> ☼ *If you need further help on editing the file, confirming the changes or exiting the vi editor, please refer to instruction on editing the 1st file.*

> ☼ *I like to indicate where I had edited the file, which is why you are seeing the line "# Added by XXX" above.*

Once you have edited both files, restart the VM.

To restart the VM, you could just power it off by closing its window, or if you prefer a more proper and managed way, to ensure there is no corrupted file, you can enter the following command at the command prompt and press [ENTER]:

```
sudo shutdown -h now
```

The screen will show the shutdown progress as follows:

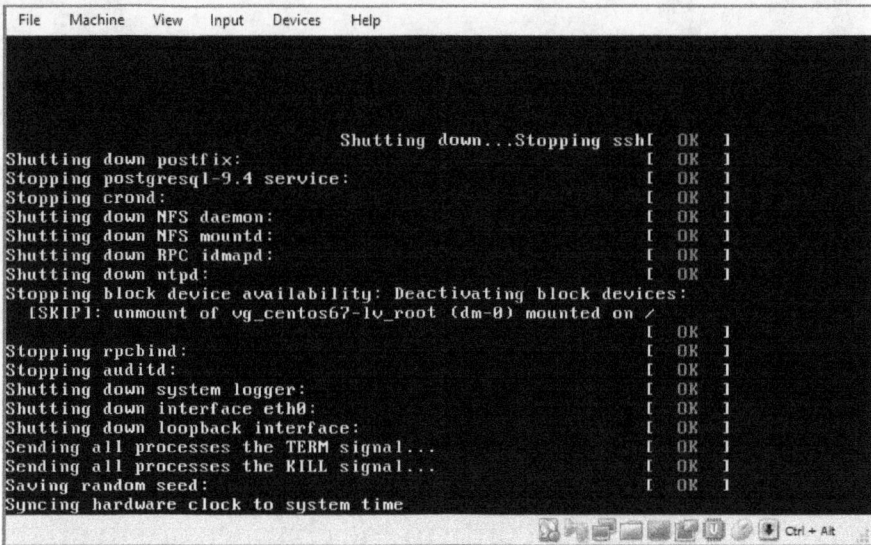

```
 File    Machine    View    Input    Devices    Help




                              Shutting down...Stopping ssh[   OK   ]
Shutting down postfix:                                 [   OK   ]
Stopping postgresql-9.4 service:                       [   OK   ]
Stopping crond:                                        [   OK   ]
Shutting down NFS daemon:                              [   OK   ]
Shutting down NFS mountd:                              [   OK   ]
Shutting down RPC idmapd:                              [   OK   ]
Shutting down ntpd:                                    [   OK   ]
Stopping block device availability: Deactivating block devices:
 [SKIP]: unmount of vg_centos67-lv_root (dm-0) mounted on /
                                                       [   OK   ]
Stopping rpcbind:                                      [   OK   ]
Stopping auditd:                                       [   OK   ]
Shutting down system logger:                           [   OK   ]
Shutting down interface eth0:                          [   OK   ]
Shutting down loopback interface:                      [   OK   ]
Sending all processes the TERM signal...               [   OK   ]
Sending all processes the KILL signal...               [   OK   ]
Saving random seed:                                    [   OK   ]
Syncing hardware clock to system time
                                                              Ctrl + Alt
```

Figure 17: VM Shutdown Screen

After that, the VM window will be closed. At this point, you have completed the PostgreSQL setup, which means that it is now able to allow DB client to connect to it.

In the next chapter, you will setup a client to connect to it.

Install a DB Client

The document provided by Pega uses DBVisualizer, you are free to use that, but personally, I prefer to use pgAdmin.

pgAdmin is the most popular and feature rich Open Source administration and development platform for PostgreSQL, which I find it more powerful and easier to use.

Just in case you are those impatient students who like to jump directly to specific chapters, please note that you need to read the prior chapter first!

You can download the pgAdmin at the following URL: https://www.pgadmin.org/download/

Alternatively, always remember that Google is your friend... 😊

For the version, I always just get the latest release version.

If you already have a version installed, there may not be a need to update to a newer version, read the release note to decide.

Install pgAdmin

The installation of pgAdmin is simple, basically just download your desired platform and version and then run the installation program.

After the installation, you should be seeing the following in the Windows Start Menu when you search for pgAdmin as shown below (your version might be slightly different):

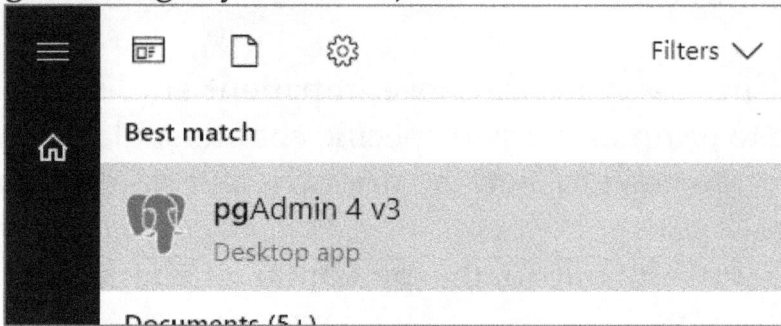

Figure 18: Searching for pgAdmin in the Start Menu

You need to launch pgAdmin from the Desktop Start Menu by clicking the icon above.

I had tried using URL link directly in the browser, but it did not work.

Configure pgAdmin

Once the pgAdmin launched in the browser, click the Servers > Create > Server as follows:

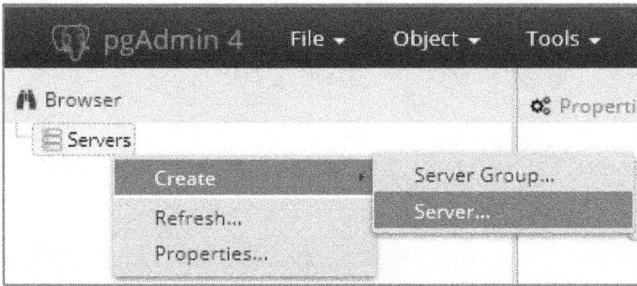

Figure 19: Creating a New Server in pgAdmin

In the dialog that pops up, under the Connection tab, enter the relevant info as follows (replace the "Host name/address" with the IP Address of your VM):

Figure 20: Connection Setting in pgAdmin

According to the document provided by the CLSA Team, the password is "postgres".

In the General tab, you may enter the information like the following:

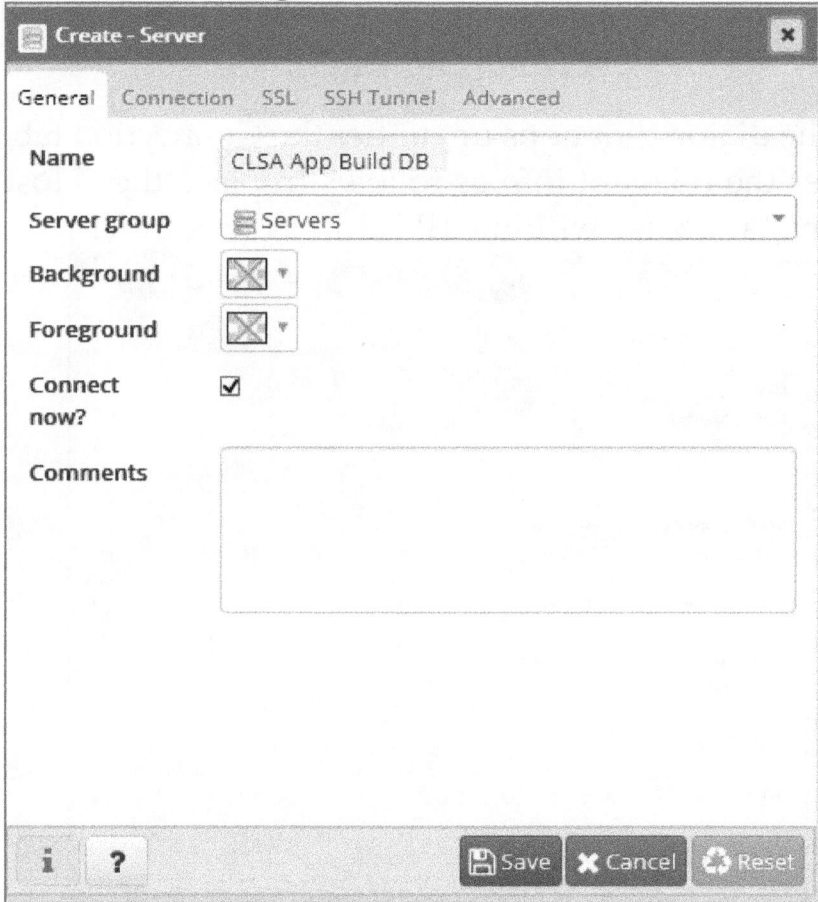

Figure 21: General Setting in pgAdmin

Tick the "Connect now?" and click the Save button.

Please make sure that your VM is already started.

If everything is ok, you should see something like the following. You can try to expand the tree to review the familiar "pegadata" and "pegarules" schemas:

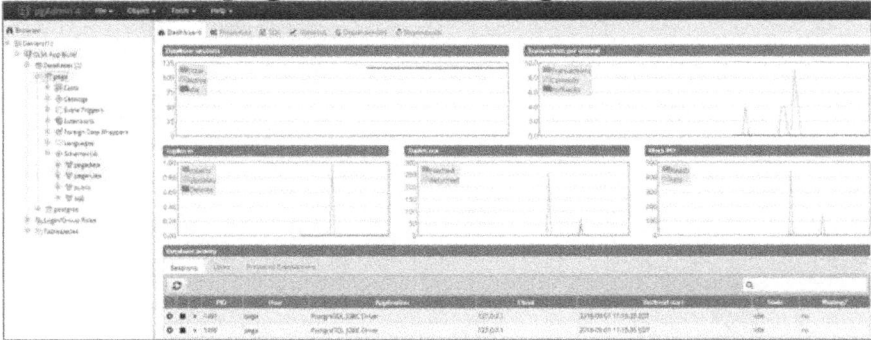

Figure 22: pgAdmin Connection Successful Screen

Do You Need to Install PuTTY?

First of all, what is PuTTY? Basically, it is just a type of command line tool that allows you to connect to the VM to issue commands.

I do not see the need as the default VM console already provided a good command line interface.

Unless you are so used to PuTTY, and like it, there is really no advantage to install that.

Personally, I cannot think of any additional features compared with the existing VM console that I feel would worth my effort to install and use it for this exam.

However, if it still up to you.

The connection parameters are as follows:

```
Hostname: [This is the IP address that is shown on
the initial VM Console screen]
Username / password: root / install
```

Install a File Transfer Program

WinSCP is a popular free SFTP and FTP client for Windows. It offers an easy to use GUI to copy files between a local and remote computer (your exam VM in this case).

To put this into your context, it basically allows you to:

1) Download the Pega log files for analysis and troubleshooting
2) Download and update any configuration files, then upload it back to the server

> Remember the earlier postgresql.conf & pg_hba.conf that you had to edit using vi editor? You can download it to your PC, edit it, and then upload it back using WinSCP! Just be careful of the NEWLINE character.

Install WinSCP
The download is available at: https://winscp.net.

Once downloaded, just run the installation program. There is really nothing special about this, it is very easy. The setup document from CLSA Team has some screenshots on the configuration screen, you can refer to that if you need more help.

Whenever, you startup WinSCP, select your desired profile and click the Login button, like the following:

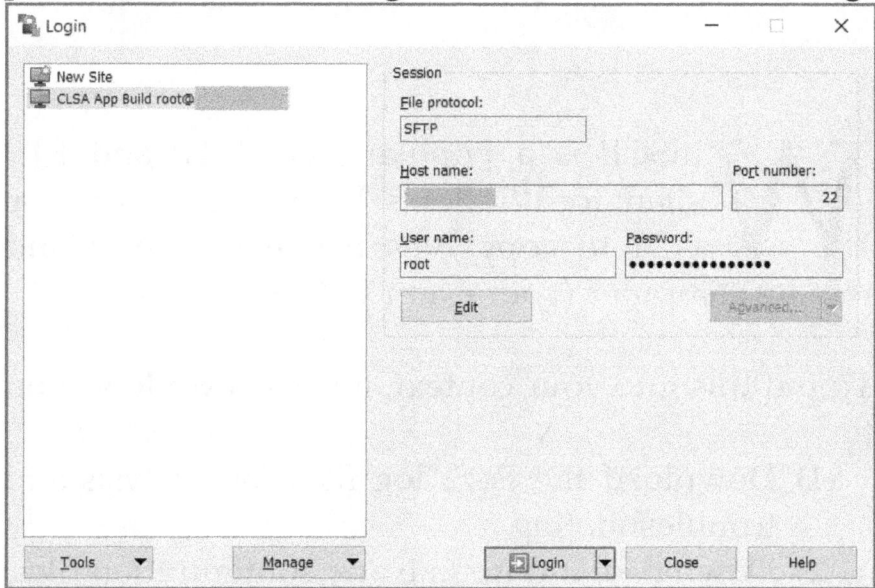

Figure 23: WinSCP Login Screen

File Paths

The following are some file paths that you should know. It is taken from the setup document itself:

Service Export Path
```
/opt/tomcat/work/Catalina/localhost/prweb/StaticConte
nt/global/ServiceExport
```
Extract Marker Folder
```
/opt/tomcat/work/Catalina/localhost/prweb
```
Config file locations
```
prconfig.xml:
/opt/tomcat/webapps/prweb/WEB-INF/classes
tomcat-users.xml:
/opt/tomcat/conf
```

```
web.xml:
/opt/tomcat/conf
```

Please don't be too overwhelmed by the settings and paths above, worrying about how to configure those.

Well, more likely than not, you would not need to touch those, at least I don't have to.

Setup the Help Files

To setup the help file, go to DESIGNER STUDIO > System > Settings > URLs. The following shows the menu navigation:

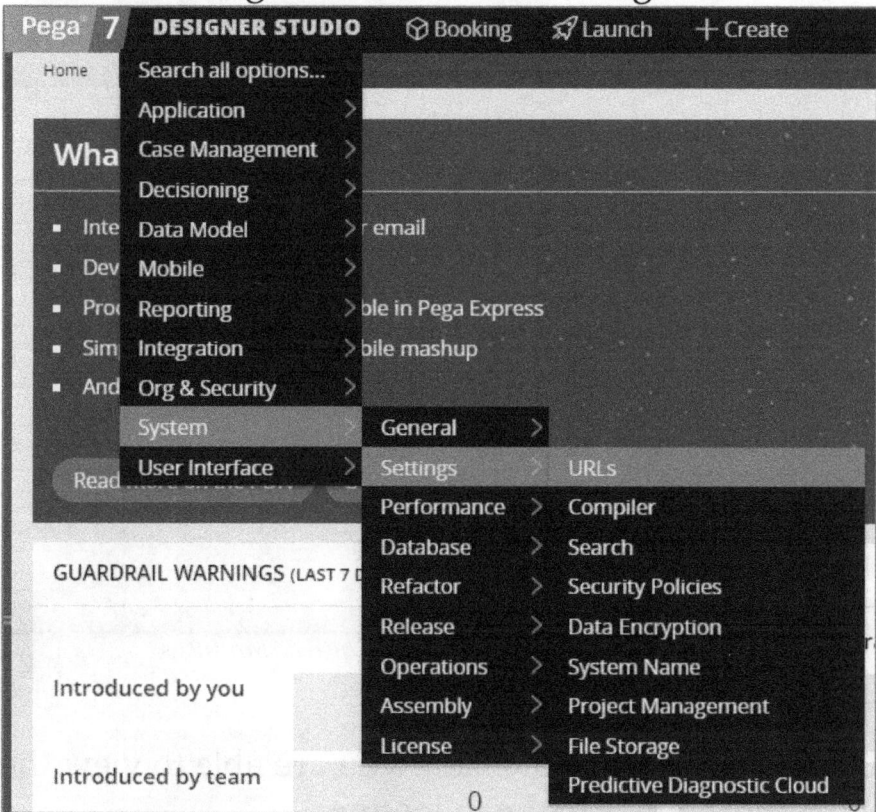

Figure 24: Menu Navigation for System URLs Settings

Once selected, the following is the settings. Provide the URL using the following format:
http://[IPAddress]:[9080]/prhelp

Click Save to save the settings as shown below.

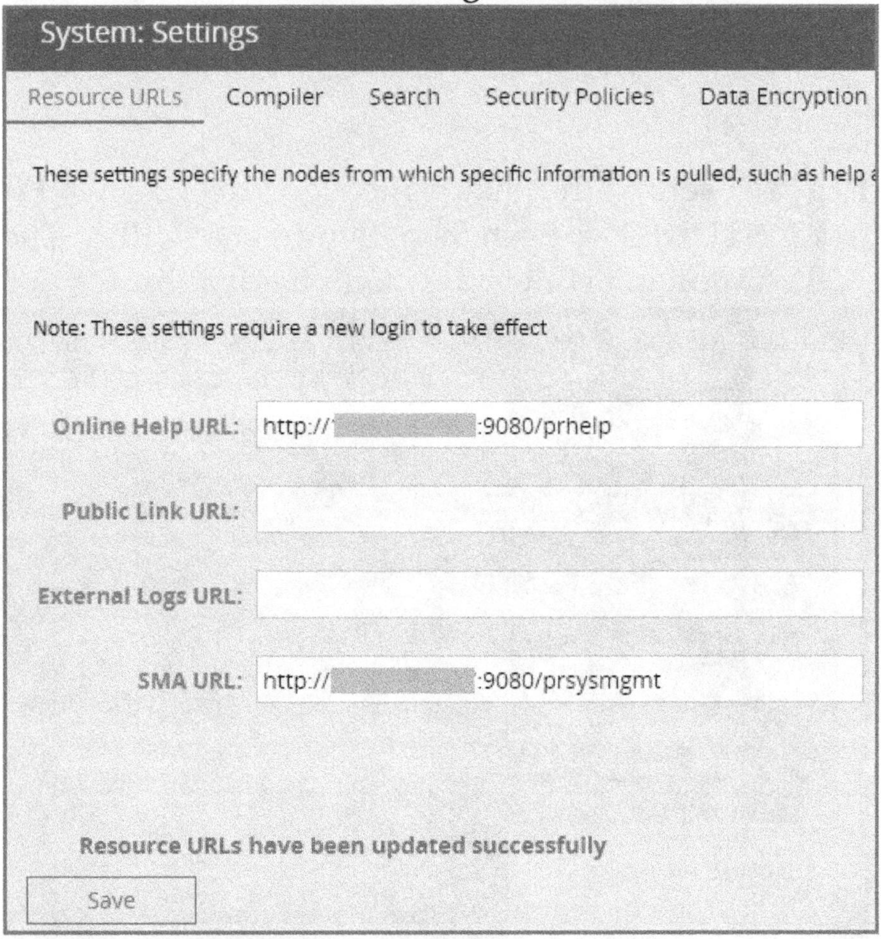

Figure 25: Configuring Online Help and SMA URLs

Test the Help Files

Access any help, make sure you are able to view the help file, similar to the following:

You are here: Case management > Case types

Case types

A case type represents work in your application that follows a life cycle, or path, to completion. By using case types, you can reuse functionality from built-on applications, manage dependencies, and automate the tasks that your team performs in real life, such as requesting approval from a manager or sending correspondence to stakeholders.

A case is an instance of a case type. Cases are created by case workers, your application, another application, or case managers who triage interaction cases.

Example case types

For example, you can define the following case types: Accident Claim, Vehicle Damage, and Bodily Injury.

A case worker creates an Accident Claim case each time a customer reports an automobile accident. After your application verifies the customer's driver's license and vehicle identification number, it creates a Vehicle Damage case that is linked to the Accident Claim case.

The case worker decides whether a Bodily Injury case is needed, based on information from the customer and the search results for similar cases. When the Vehicle Damage and Bodily Injury cases are processed by other case workers, the funds payable and updated policy premium are stored in the Accident Claim case.

A case manager is then notified that the Accident Claim is ready for review.

※ **Related information**
- Creating a hierarchy of case types

Figure 26: Example of Accessing the Help File URL

You should also configure the SMA URL at the same time. The URL is shown above.

Setup Pega SMA

Based on the URL that you have entered in the setting above, open the SMA URL in Internet Explorer (IE).

In the left panel, click the "+" sign to add a new node and configure it as follows:

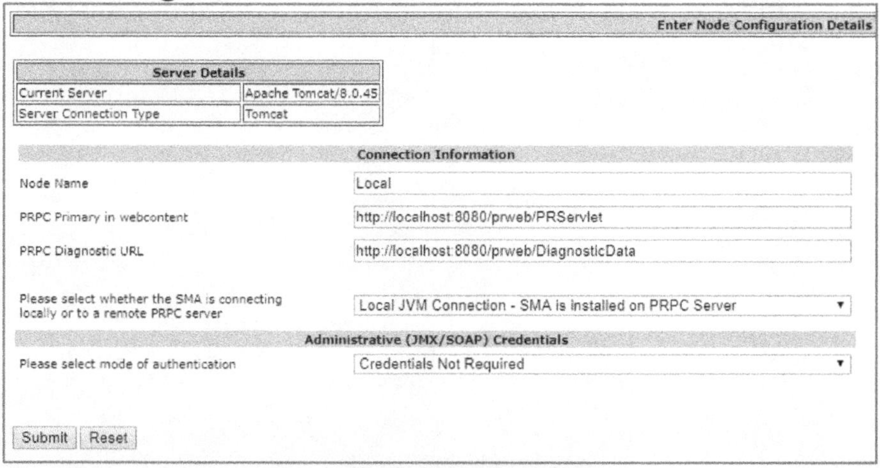

Figure 27: Configuration of SMA

Click the Submit button to save the settings.

Test the Configuration

To test the configuration, click on the node name in the left panel that you have setup earlier, you should see something like the following:

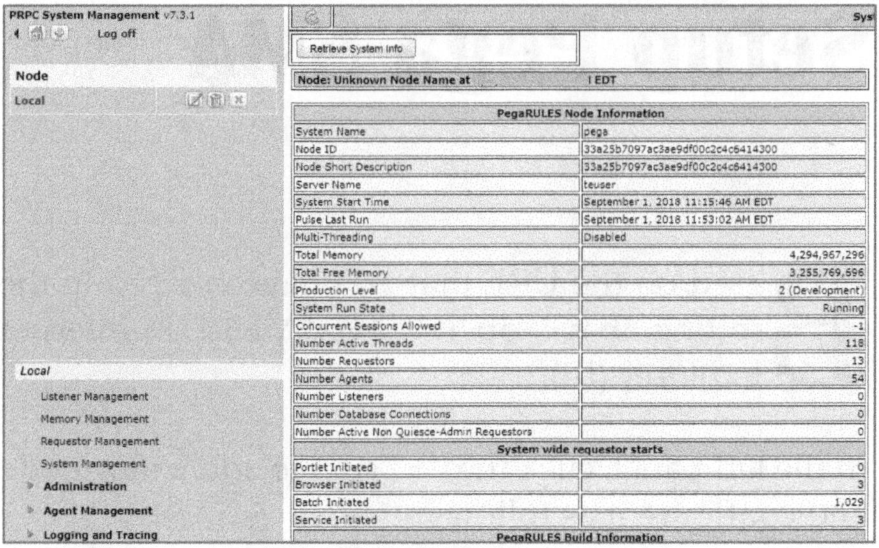

PRPC System Management v7.3.1				Sys
◀ 🖻 💾 Log off				

Retrieve System Info	

Node	

Node: Unknown Node Name at	I EDT

Local	🗏 🗑 ✕

PegaRULES Node Information	
System Name	pega
Node ID	33a25b7097ac3ae9df00c2c4c6414300
Node Short Description	33a25b7097ac3ae9df00c2c4c6414300
Server Name	teuser
System Start Time	September 1, 2018 11:15:46 AM EDT
Pulse Last Run	September 1, 2018 11:53:02 AM EDT
Multi-Threading	Disabled
Total Memory	4,294,967,296
Total Free Memory	3,255,769,696
Production Level	2 (Development)
System Run State	Running
Concurrent Sessions Allowed	-1
Number Active Threads	118
Number Requestors	13
Number Agents	54
Number Listeners	0
Number Database Connections	0
Number Active Non Quiesce-Admin Requestors	0
System wide requestor starts	
Portlet Initiated	0
Browser Initiated	3
Batch Initiated	1,029
Service Initiated	3
PegaRULES Build Information	

Left navigation:

Local

- Listener Management
- Memory Management
- Requestor Management
- System Management
- ▶ Administration
- ▶ Agent Management
- ▶ Logging and Tracing

Figure 28: Testing the SMA Configuration

Access the Log Files

The easiest way to access the log file is via the Designer Studio > System > Operations > Logs, as shown below:

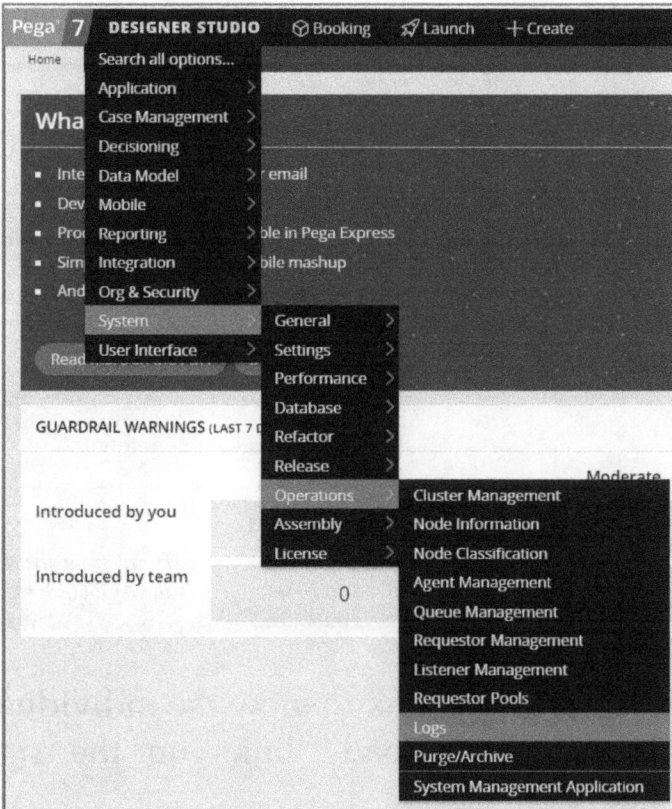

Figure 29: Accessing the Log File Through Designer Studio

In the following screen, click the "Log files".

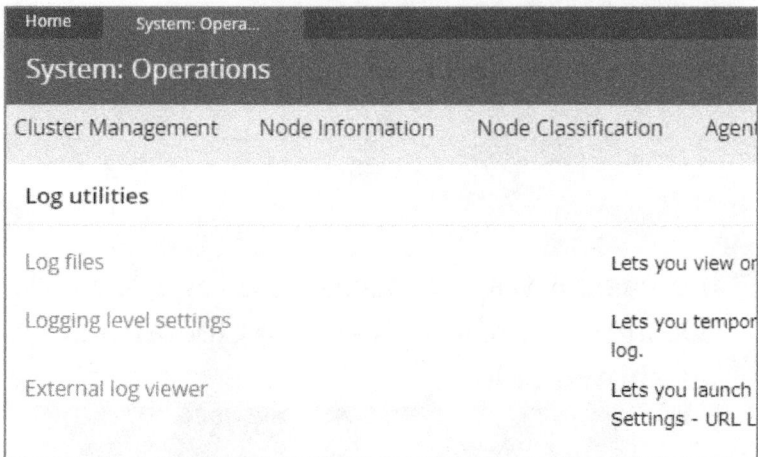

Figure 30: System Operations - Log Utilities

The above will pop up a link showing you all the log files as follows:

Appender	File (click to view)	Download
BIX	/opt/tomcat/work/Catalina/localhost/prweb/PegaBIX.log	text or zip
SECURITYEVENT	/opt/tomcat/work/Catalina/localhost/prweb/PegaRULES-SecurityEvent.log	text or zip
ALERTSECURITY	/opt/tomcat/work/Catalina/localhost/prweb/PegaRULES-ALERTSECURITY.log	text or zip
PEGA	/opt/tomcat/work/Catalina/localhost/prweb/PegaRULES.log	text or zip
ALERT	/opt/tomcat/work/Catalina/localhost/prweb/PegaRULES-ALERT.log	text or zip
CLUSTER	/opt/tomcat/work/Catalina/localhost/prweb/PegaCLUSTER.log	text or zip
(all logs)		zip

Close

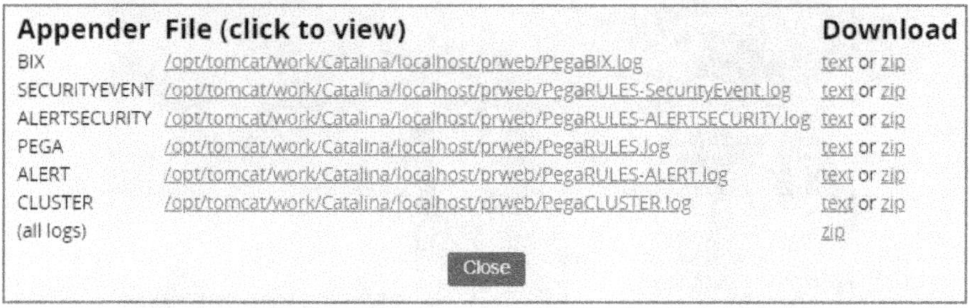

Figure 31: List of Log Files From Designer Studio

You will notice that the log file screen above is different from the document provided to you. This is because what I have here is the ACTUAL screen from the VM. The earlier pdf sent was outdated.

You can click on the link to view the individual files or click the "Download" links on the right to download it.

If you would like to download it, the username and password are both [admin].

Alternatively, you can use WinSCP to navigate to the respective path to download the files to your machine.

Inspecting the Log Files

Before you do anything, it is always wise to inspect the log files, and take a backup copy, why?

The reason is simple: You do not want to confuse the 'OOTB errors' with the errors of yours.

Imaging that you were having an issue, and while trying to figure out what is wrong, you saw a bunch of errors in the log file. Wouldn't that be demoralising and confusing for you?

The following was my log file, so far so good.

```
] (ervlet.WebAppLifeCycleListener) INFO   - PegaRULES Web Tier 7.3.1
] (ervlet.WebAppLifeCycleListener) INFO   - PRPC-7.3.1-184: 2017-10-14 00.41 E
] (ervlet.WebAppLifeCycleListener) INFO   - prpc-platform.git (2dba5f1abf39c01
] (ervlet.WebAppLifeCycleListener) INFO   - Now starting the PegaRULES Web Tie
] (    context.web.WebEnvironment) INFO   - Web tier using local JNDI context

] (  priv.context.JNDIEnvironment) INFO   - Web-tier default Engine bean name
] (les.internal.ModulesBridgeImpl) INFO   - Initializing engine modules.
] (nal.DefaultConfigurationSource) INFO   - prconfig.xml merged with prconfig
] (able.DefaultVirtualTableConfig) INFO   - Using Hybrid Virtual Rules Table i
] (able.DefaultVirtualTableConfig) INFO   - VTable dispatches rules for 7 Aspe
] (able.DefaultVirtualTableConfig) INFO   - ABA[AC] dispatches rules for 1 Asp
] (  priv.context.JNDIEnvironment) INFO   - Enterprise-tier default Engine bea
] (r.context.EtierEnvironmentImpl) INFO   - Enterprise tier using local JNDI c

] (ion.internal.PRGenProviderImpl) INFO   - invokeDynamic instrumentation for
] (ion.internal.PRGenProviderImpl) INFO   - Assembly Version: 762781845
] (dbms.JdbcConnectionManagerImpl) INFO   - Initializing connections for pegar
] (       external.timers.CpuTimer) INFO   - CPU timers set to TOTALSONLY. Use
] (.timers.EnvironmentDiagnostics) INFO   - Using Java 1.5 Thread.getAllStackT
] (.access.PageDatabaseMapperImpl) INFO   - DeflateStreams is turned ON.
] (pboard.StorageStreamCommonImpl) INFO   - engineCodeVersion: 07-10-33
] ( internal.archive.ParUtilsImpl) INFO   - Setting archive staging directory:
] (      etier.impl.EngineStartup) INFO   - JVM Information:
] (      etier.impl.EngineStartup) INFO   -    Vendor: Oracle Corporation, JVM
] (      etier.impl.EngineStartup) INFO   -    VM Name: Java HotSpot(TM) 64-Bi
] (      etier.impl.EngineStartup) INFO   - Host OS Information:
] (      etier.impl.EngineStartup) INFO   -    OS: Linux, version: 2.6.32-696.
```

Figure 32: Sample Pega Log File

However, I am seeing these errors:

```
20XX-XX-XX 12:47:37,300 [                        teuser] [    STANDARD]
[                        ] [                                            ]
(uster.internal.ClusterProvider)  ERROR    - Error fetching this
machine's ip address (InetAddress.getLocalHost()), falling back to
'localhost'
java.net.UnknownHostException: pega7: pega7: Name or service not
known
        at
java.net.InetAddress.getLocalHost(InetAddress.java:1505)
~[?:1.8.0_141]
        at
com.pega.platform.cluster.internal.AbstractClusterProvider.start(
AbstractClusterProvider.java:99) ~[cluster.jar:?]
        at
com.pega.platform.cluster.management.internal.DefaultClusterManag
er.start(DefaultClusterManager.java:114) ~[cluster.jar:?]
```

Figure 33: Sample OOTB Errors in Log File

Anyway, I just did a backup of the files and ignore those.

Performing Re-Indexing of Search Index

In general, this should be a simple task, You can access this using: Designer Studio > System > Settings > Search, as shown below:

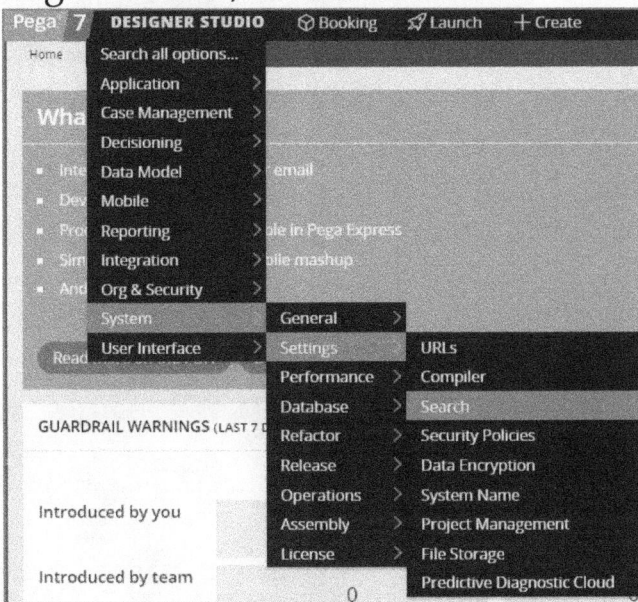

Figure 34: Accessing Pega Search Index

As you would again realise, the steps provided in the CLSA document is not updated. ☹

Anyway, after clicking the menu item, you would see the following:

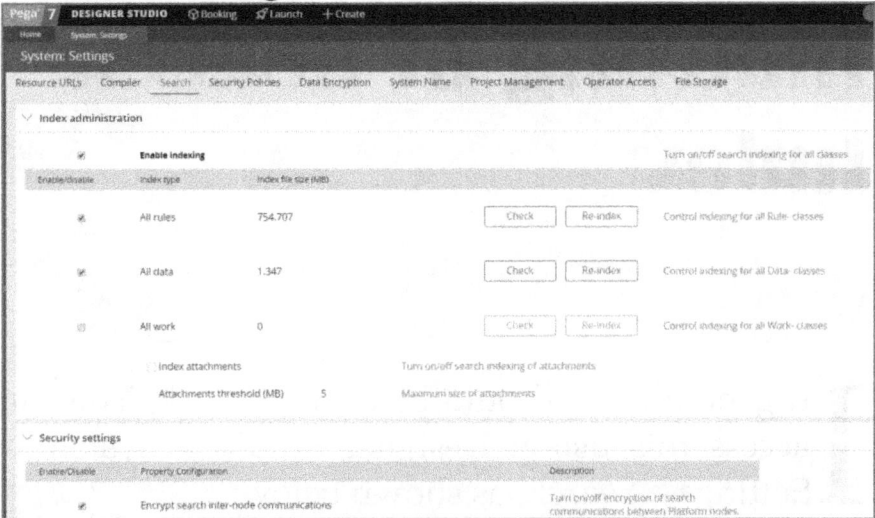

Figure 35: Pega Search Index Screen

There is really no magic here, basically, just scroll down and take note of the following:

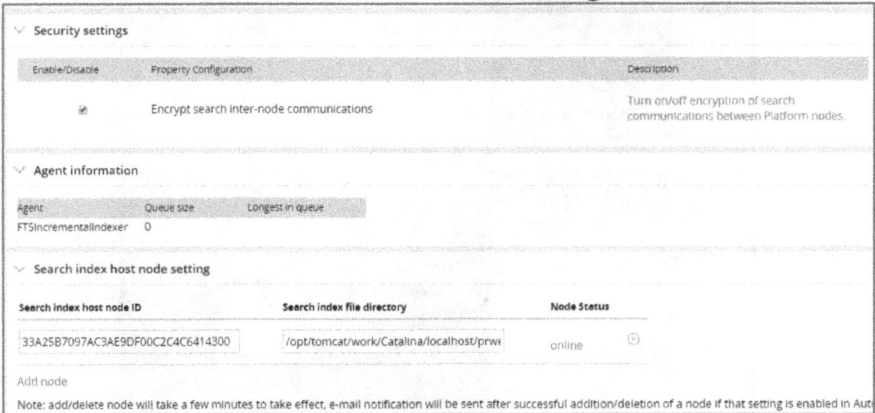

Figure 36: Search Index Agent Information and Search Index Host Node Setting

For the "Agent information" section, take note that the Queue size MUST be zero, if it is not, then very likely, you are having some agent issue. Ask the Pega

Community for help or contact CLSA Team. The other important section is "Search index host node setting". You need to ensure that the "Node Status" is "online", as shown above. If it is not, again, shout for help!

Scroll back to the top, and under the "Index administration" section, ensure the indexes are enabled.

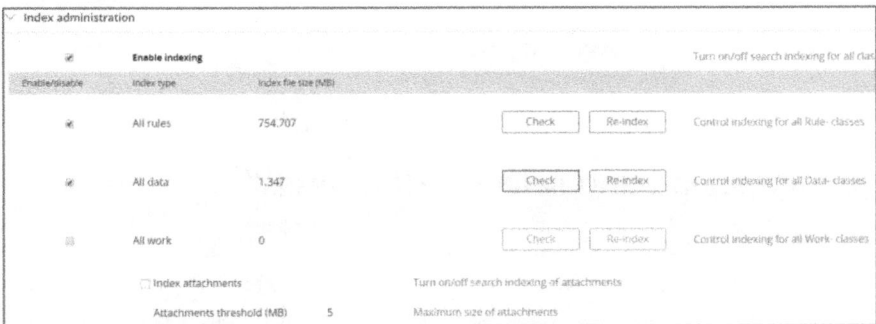

Figure 37: Index Administration with Core Indexes Enabled

By default, the "All work" is not ticked. This does not really matter.

Click the Check button one-by-one, make sure you have a message indication that all are well as shown below:

Figure 38: Diagnostic Messages of the Search Indexes

If you are curious, you can always try to click the "Re-index" button, and you should see this:

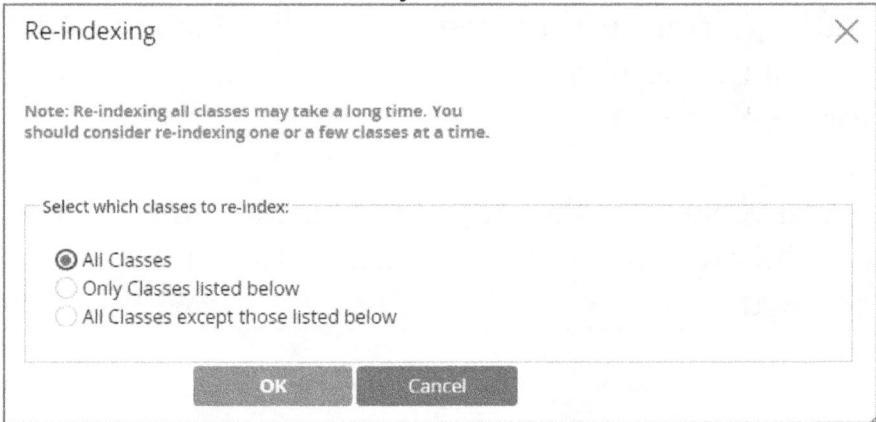

Figure 39:Re-Indexing Dialog Box

Just go ahead and select "All Classes".

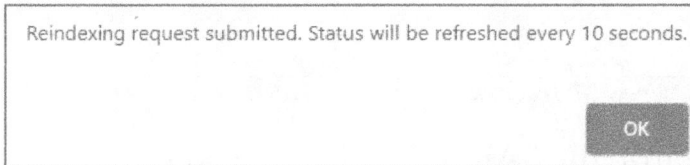

Figure 40: Re-Indexing Confirmation Window

Observe the index, it should be progressing as shown below:

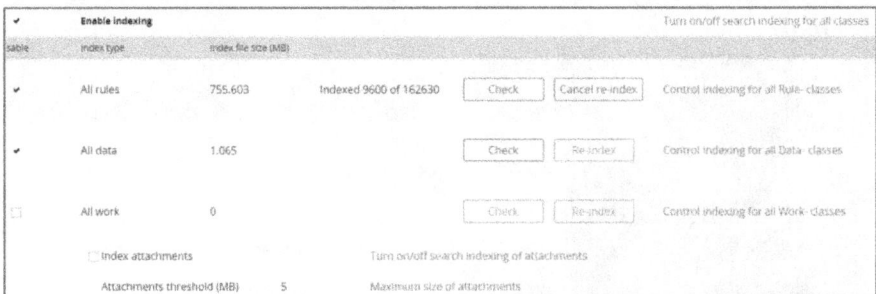

Figure 41: Re-Indexing in Progress

Once everything is done, you will be back to the screen, showing the completed index sizes.

Of course, Murphy's Law applies, if it is not broken, don't fix it, unless you have a lot of time to play around with it.

Choose a More Reliable VM Networking

During my application build, my network was disconnected a few times, for no reason at all. In fact, I had NEVER encountered such issue before, and the application build was my first encounter! (Murphy's law)

At that time, I didn't want to make any changes to my VM, including the network, so I had waited, logout, login and also restarted the VM. The issue continued, and I persisted, but in the end, Tomcat was corrupted, and I couldn't even access the Designer Studio. This was the error screen:

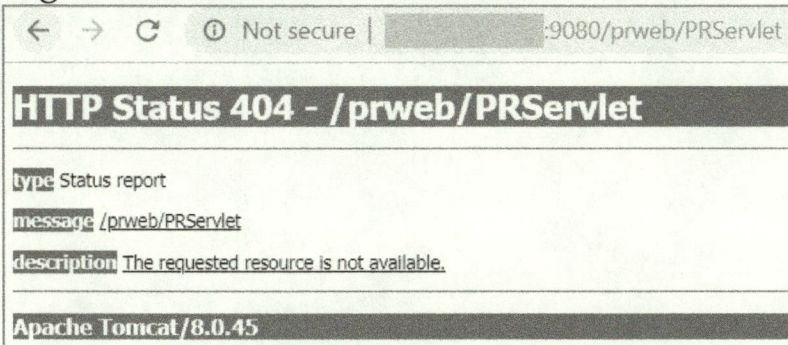

Figure 42: Unable to Access Designer Studio, Tomcat Error

Wasn't that horrific? My application build VM could no longer be accessed! Which meant that I could no longer continue my application build!!! ☹

 Till today, I still did not have any idea what went wrong.

I didn't use host-only adapter initially as I was not sure if there would be a need to connect to the Internet from the VM.

In the end, I had to change the VM network to Host-Only adapter and continue my exams after restoring my snapshot.

That leads us to the next point...

Do Multiple Snapshots of Your Application Build Solution

Yes, like the advice I gave for the exercise solutions, I am again advising you to do multiple snapshots for your application build solution too.

So how many is appropriate? In general, whenever you have any sizable implementation, you should do a snapshot.

Another point you need to be aware is that it is cleaner and easier if you do a snapshot while the system is in the shutdown state. This makes copying to another machine to continue your work much easier.

The following is my actual snapshot of the application build.

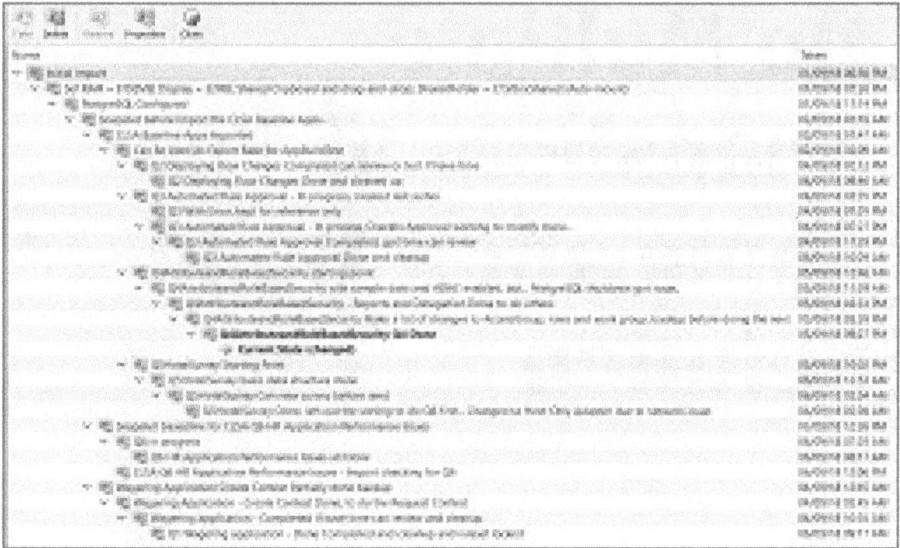

Figure 43: Samples Application Build VM Snapshots (Redacted)

I am not shy to show you the massive work that I did, in fact, I am proud. 😊

It was because I was so careful and diligent, which ultimately helped me to pass the application build on the 1st attempt.

Another advantage of multiple snapshots is that if you are stuck in a question, you can always snapshot it, put some comments, and move on to other questions first.

In general, before you start the application build, you should create a Master VM that has all the starting points for all the questions.

Note that the questions are unrelated, and you are expected to package them in a way that there would be no dependence.

> *There are multiple questions and they are totally unrelated, and you are expected to submit each solution as separate packages (full standalone). Of course, this might change, so always validate the requirements and expectations of the application build.*

Create Windows Shortcuts

In the application build, you would want to have all the information ready. Therefore, creating some shortcuts would really help.

For me, I have created shortcuts on my start menu for the VM, pgAdmin, as well as for the WinSCP, as shown below:

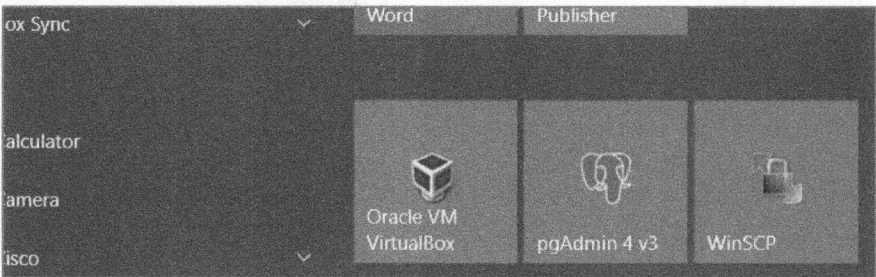

Figure 44: Start Menu Shortcuts

For my file system, I have a shortcut to all my design documents and backup of the exported codes, at my fingertips, using the "Quick access" feature.

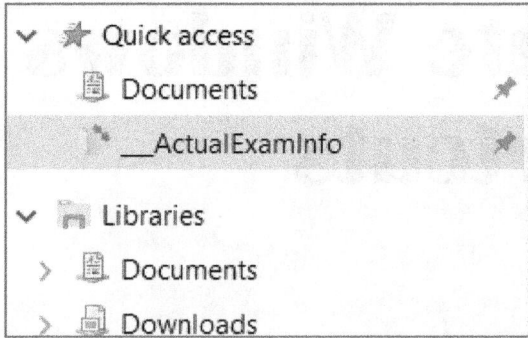

Figure 45: Windows Explorer Quick Access Feature

Prepare the Share Links and the Email

For submission of your application build, you need to send an email to CLSA Team, with links to your packages, as well as to attach the design documents for all the questions.

Configure the Share Links

First of all, DO NOT share the document link! This is because if you happen to update the package file, the link will change, and you will need to update the document link reference again!

Worst, if you forgot to update the link, the examiner is either going to get your older version or no file at all! Marks are definitely going to be deducted.

Therefore, in your share drive, e.g. Google Drive, DropBox, or whatever, create a main folder, called CLSA Application Build, and within it, create subfolders for each question. After that, generate the share link for each of the question folders.

In most share drive, you can configure a custom URL for your download. In Box, this is the setting page:

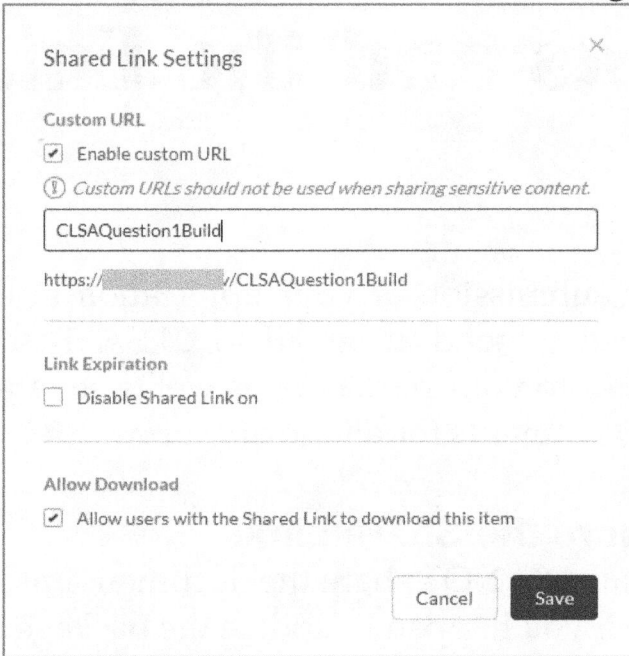

Shared Link Settings   ×

Custom URL
☑ Enable custom URL
ⓘ *Custom URLs should not be used when sharing sensitive content.*

> CLSAQuestion1Build

https://_____/CLSAQuestion1Build

Link Expiration
☐ Disable Shared Link on

Allow Download
☑ Allow users with the Shared Link to download this item

Cancel   Save

Figure 46: Creating Custom Shared Link in Box

Use this link instead, to embed into your email. Now, whenever you have updates, you can just upload to this folder, replacing the earlier.

There will ensure that the examiner would always be able to get your latest file! 😊

See, another uncertainty is taken out of the equation!

Prepare the Submission Email

Yes, you can prepare the submission email beforehand.

The most important thing is to remember to include your candidate ID in the email subject.

The following is a draft:

```
Subject: CLSA Application Build Submission (Candidate
ID: XXXXX)

Hi CLSA Team,
Attached is the submission for the above:

Q1 - XXX XXX
[https://xxx.xxx.com/Q1Submission]
Q2 - XXX XXX
[https://xxx.xxx.com/Q2Submission]
Q3 - XXX XXX
[https://xxx.xxx.com/Q3Submission]
Q4 - XXX XXX
[https://xxx.xxx.com/Q4Submission]
Q5 - XXX XXX
[https://xxx.xxx.com/Q5Submission]
Q6 - XXX XXX
[https://xxx.xxx.com/Q6Submission]

Thanks and please confirm receipt of this submission.

Regards,
[Your Name]
```

Figure 47: Sample Submission Email

Your Candidate ID is the last 5 digits of your Pearson VUE Candidate ID. Just look at any of your Pearson Vue score report, you will see that.

Remember, your submission packages (.zip or .jar) must also contain your candidate ID.

If you are worried that you might 'type' your candidate ID wrongly, just reply to the CLSA Team's acknowledgment email, which also contains your candidate ID.

Practice Packaging the Application

Although not something that is difficult, please practice this before the exam. You need to know 3 ways of packaging the application.

The 3 ways I am referring to are:
- Packaging an Application
- Packaging Ruleset Versions
- Packaging Individual Rules

Packaging an Application
This is basically running the application wizard, most of the time, you will just take all the default.

Use this method if you are told to create an application from scratch.

Packaging Ruleset Versions
Use this if you are performing some fixes, adding new features to an existing application, etc.

With this, just create a RUP and specify the ruleset versions.

Note that some of the rules might not be in the ruleset version, in this case, you would need to manually package those individual rules.

Packaging Individual Rules

Some rules are not in the ruleset versions, thus you would need to manually add them into the package.

The key point is to get the pzInsKey of the rule that you want to package.

To do that, open that rule. Click on the Actions > View XML, then search for the pzInsKey, and copy that into the RUP.

Don't assume your package would work OOTB, always have a blank environment to import and test it, just like what your examiner would do!

Even if you are 100% certain that your distribution package will work OOTB upon importing, I would still suggest that you always include setup and configuration instructions, just in case it wouldn't! Including setup and configuration is an acceptable practice. Don't risk losing points by assuming too much!

Conclusion

I have given you all the tips and the procedures that I took, as well as the purposes for all those extra works. But do you really have to do all those preparations? It is massive! 🙁

Do I Have to Do All These?

Well, if you know what would happen and what would not, then you just need to prepare for those events that would affect you. Unfortunately, this is not the case in real-life!

If I were given the knowledge of today, travel back in time into the past to take the CLSA application build, I would still do all of what I did and documented here.

This is because I only want to do it once... and do it good... There is really no point in taking risks that has no proportional returns. Logical, right? 😊

Therefore, it is entirely up to you to decide how well prepared you want to be, bear in mind that you would not know what could happen, so being well prepared is the best thing that you can do for yourself!

What Are Those That Would Really Help Me?

However, to be fair to those who are really pressed for time and couldn't afford to do everything (for whatever reasons), it is only fair that I give you more insights.

1) First and foremost: Choose a good starting time and location to do your application build
2) Fix the Inherent VM issue
3) Get good machines. Either a single powerful machine or 2 that can run 2 VMs at the same time
4) Do multiple snapshots of the exercise systems as well as your application build
5) Practice packaging the application. You should know how to use all the 3 methods
6) Prepare all your submission email and the share drive links well in advance
7) Do the DB connection setup

Please refer to the respective sections on the procedure to accomplish the above and the motivation of those.

What Is Next?

Going through this book will ensure that you are well prepared, and nothing 'unfortunate' should prevent you from continuing the application build.

When I was teaching and writing course materials, I had come across a lot of students, who know the answer, but their presentations indicated otherwise.

There are also other students, who are very smart, but ended up 'imagining' too much and 'interpreted' the questions with so much complexity that they ended up failing it.

These are all very sad situations.

This is the 1st book in this series. Look out for other books, which I will go into more details on how to tackle open-ended exams questions. In our case, the Pega CLSA application build.

The following are some of the important skills that you should learn:
- How to Analyse the Question
- How to Answer the Question
- How to Present Your Answer

We will dive into that in the next series.

So, do you want to be my virtual undergraduate student? If you do, then follow me on this journey!

URL: https://www.DebunkumBeaver.com
Twitter: @DebunkumBeaver

Hurry, lesson is about to begin! 😊

Good luck and all the best for your exams and remember to check back for more information!

www.ingramcontent.com/pod-product-compliance
Lightning Source LLC
Chambersburg PA
CBHW021107210326
41598CB00016B/1369